Inside the Rainbow
Volume 2

First published in Great Britain in 2022 by Piquant Editions

piquanteditions.com

British Library Cataloguing-in-Publication Data
A catalogue record for this book is available from the British Library

ISBN: 978-1-80329-003-4

Cover Painting: *The holy Quadriga* by Pieter Kwant (2022)
Cover design: Projectluz.com

This book was painted and written with Elria,
for

Dave & Heather, Josh & Lauren,
Barnes & Beth, Tim & Nomes,
as well as

Susie, Isla, Dougal,
Lucas, Ciara, Heidi,
Zahra, Ava,
Saoirse, Jonah and Hudson.

Dedicated, with special thanks, to the Langham "family" who granted me a three-month sabbatical to finish this volume.

"Our Father in heaven,
Reveal who you are.
Set the world right;
Do what's best –
as above, so below."

Matthew 6:9–10 (The Message)

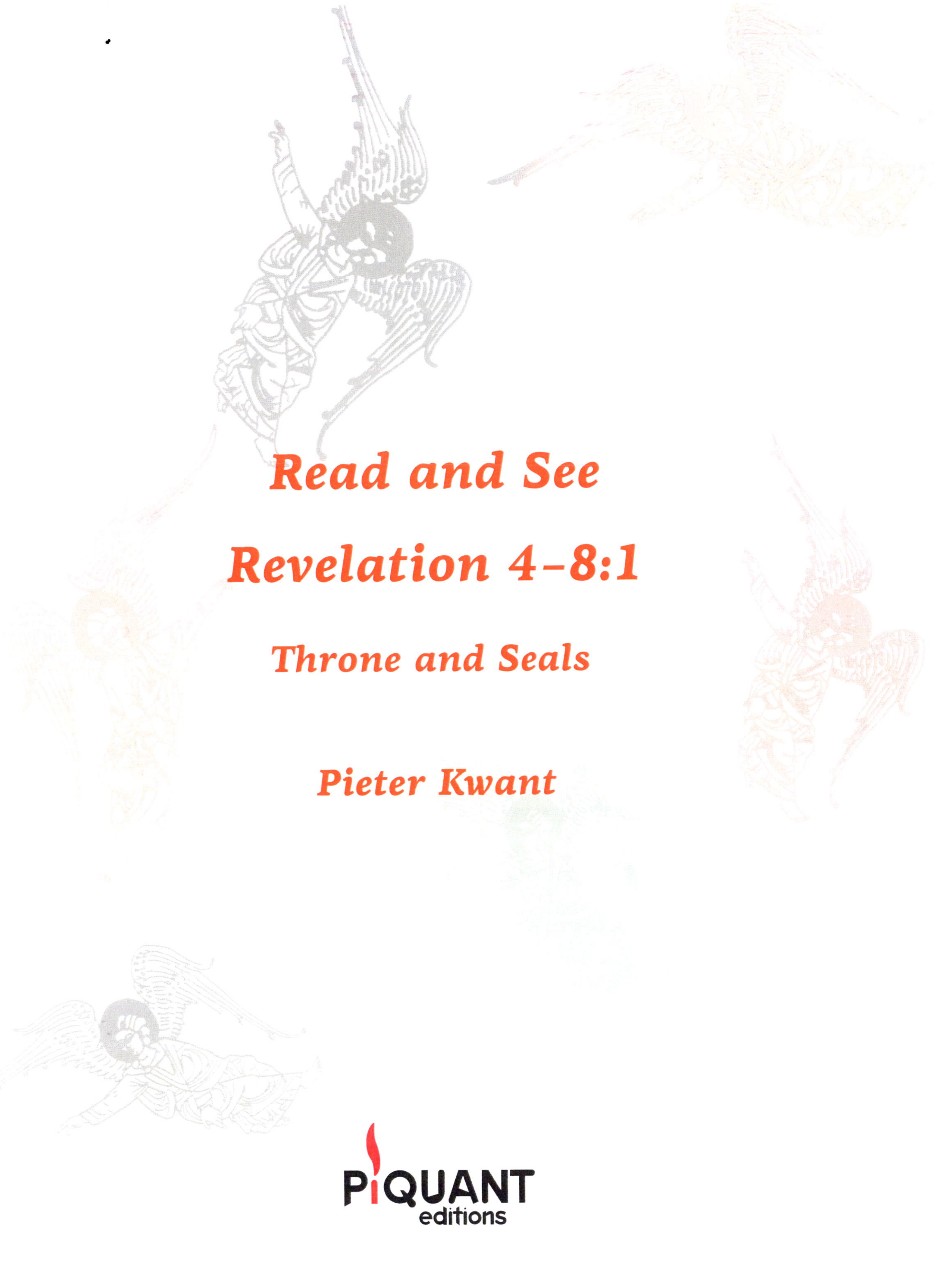

Read and See Revelation 4–8:1

Throne and Seals

Pieter Kwant

PIQUANT editions

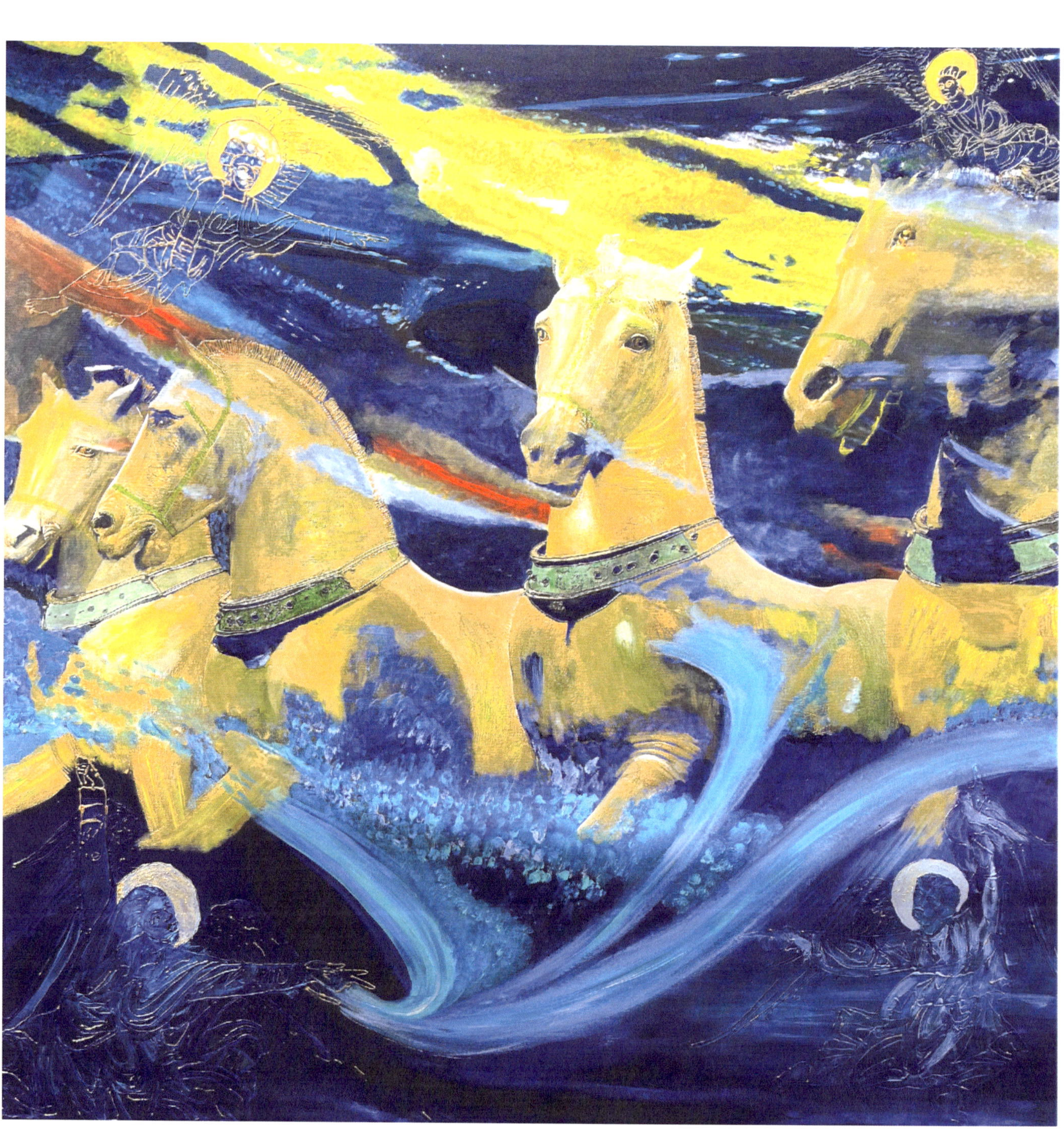

A Way of Reading

The main challenge of Revelation is how to read it! When comparing early commentators like Victorinus, Bede and Tyconius with more recent Charles, Bauckham and Caird, it is often hard to believe they even refer to the same text!

So, why are there such vastly different ways of reading it? Because of different worldviews, including different traditions of how to read texts. For example, Tyconius developed seven rules for reading in a "spiritual" manner. Many modern commentators dismiss "spiritual" or "allegorical" readings in favour of "literary" and "critical" ones. You can find more about this in the bibliography.[1]

Quadriga is a Latin word for the team of four horses that pulled Roman chariots. It became shorthand for a method of biblical interpretation used by the church fathers and throughout the Middle Ages: first, the literal meaning of the text; second, the allegorical or spiritual; third, the moral (tropological); and fourth, the anagogical (dealing with the future). Wikipedia has this translation of a Latin rhyme used to memorize it:

> The literal teaches what God and our ancestors did,
> The allegory is where our faith and belief are hid,
> The moral meaning gives us the rule of daily life,
> The anagoge shows us where we end our strife.

When I read this, I was meditating on how to portray the four horses of the apocalypse. One of my daughters-in-law at the same time commissioned a painting from me in blue and gold. As she also loves horses, I realized I could combine the two! The result is on the opposite page (and on the cover), but not to portray the horses of the apocalypse! I quote the four bronze horses of St. Mark's Basilica in Venice, formerly in the Hippodrome of Constantinople (1204). (The original is now in a museum and since 1980 a replica graces St. Mark's). While I was painting these horses, they "turned" gold. Blues and yellows create the movement initiated by the four *Beatus* angels (whom you met in my first book). I like to be reminded that the supernatural is always here, with us, right now. Revelation in particular so clearly teaches this! (I am delighted that my family welcomed the painting; and I hope it will be a quiet reminder that the Bible, and our lives, have these layers of meaning that all need attention.)

Can we apply the Quadriga method today, in our instant society? For me, this method of Bible interpretation has become a small apocalypse, or "unveiling", in itself. Following Leithart's guidance, for example, "Literally, Jerusalem is the city of David; allegorically, it is the church; tropologically, each of us is a city in which God dwells, so what applies to the whole city applies to each of us; anagogically it is the future [new] Jerusalem."

The "horse of the literal and historical" meaning of the text: to read the text, what it says and affirms, look at its literary form, its context, how it tells the story and connects the narrative. For example, "Literally, Jerusalem is the city of David" (Leithart).

The "horse of faith": how does the passage relate to Jesus, as revealed in the Old and New Testaments? In my protestant tradition I would seek a more typological spiritual understanding: how do the words I read connect me to Jesus, point to Him and, most importantly, unveil Him?

The "horse of love": what does the text encourage us to do, to be, to become in Christ? How does it encourage us to relate to Him and to others, our neighbours? How do we DO Revelation?

The "horse of hope": what does our biblical future look like? In Revelation the future vision of the new Jerusalem is used to encourage the seven churches in their challenges. The future joy Jesus has promised becomes the motivation for their faith and love: driven by hope not by law. Already glimmers of the new Jerusalem are starting to shine through ...

The four horses move in unison; they pull the chariot with equal strength. In the same way, our interpretation of the text needs to give equal attention to all four principles. When one horse runs ahead, it causes chaos: important to remember as we read Revelation with its many layers of meaning. The horses are "controlled" by ceaseless prayer, worship and wonder.

---

1 There are a number of works that helped me get a grip on this. First, a doctoral thesis on Tyconius by David Charles Robinson, *The Mystic Rules of Scripture: Tyconius of Carthage's keys and windows to the Apocalypse*. It opened my eyes to why those early commentaries were so different, and how to appreciate the seven rules. Secondly, Daniel K. Darko's *Against Principalities and Powers*. This opened my eyes to how the spirit world was perceived by both the early readers and the NT writers and exposed my own post-modern world view (and that of the many modern commentators). Finally and most importantly, Leithart's two-volume commentary on *Revelation*. I found him the first protestant modern commentator who considered all the early and later commentators seriously. Also, in his "deep exegesis" he very helpfully suggests a reinstatement of the Quadriga way of biblical interpretation.

The Throne in Heaven

The first vision (in Story Fifteen, *Rainbow* 1) ended with words to Laodicea: "To the one who conquers, I will give a place with me on my throne, just as I myself conquered and sat down with my Father on his throne." John continues seamlessly into a second vision that looks into heaven itself. He sees an open door (in Rev 3, a door was closed!). He sees a throne, and every detail is described in relation to that throne. The "one" who is seated on the throne is not named (as yet) but described in terms of glory: like *iaspis* and *sardius* within an *iris* (a bow). The "bow" can refer to a warrior's bow (bow and arrow) or a rainbow. It shines like *smaragdos*.

Who is the one on the throne? Those who surround the throne will tell us (4:8,11): He is God, the thrice-Holy one, the one Who-Is-and-who-Was-and-who-Is-To-Come, the Almighty one.

I set my painting in a liturgical context, based on the inside of Westminster Abbey in Mission, Canada. The trumpets depict

4: [1]After this I looked, and there in heaven a door stood
open! And the first voice, which I had heard speaking to
me like a trumpet, said, "Come up here, and I will show
you what must take place after this." [2]At once I was in
the spirit, and there in heaven stood a throne, with one
seated on the throne! [3]And the one seated there looks
like jasper and carnelian, and around the throne is a
rainbow that looks like an emerald. [4]Around the throne
are twenty-four thrones, and seated on the thrones
are twenty-four elders, dressed in white robes, with
golden crowns on their heads. [5]Coming from the throne
are flashes of lightning, and rumblings and peals of
thunder, and in front of the throne burn seven flam-
ing torches, which are the seven spirits of God; [6]and
in front of the throne there is something like a sea of
glass, like crystal.

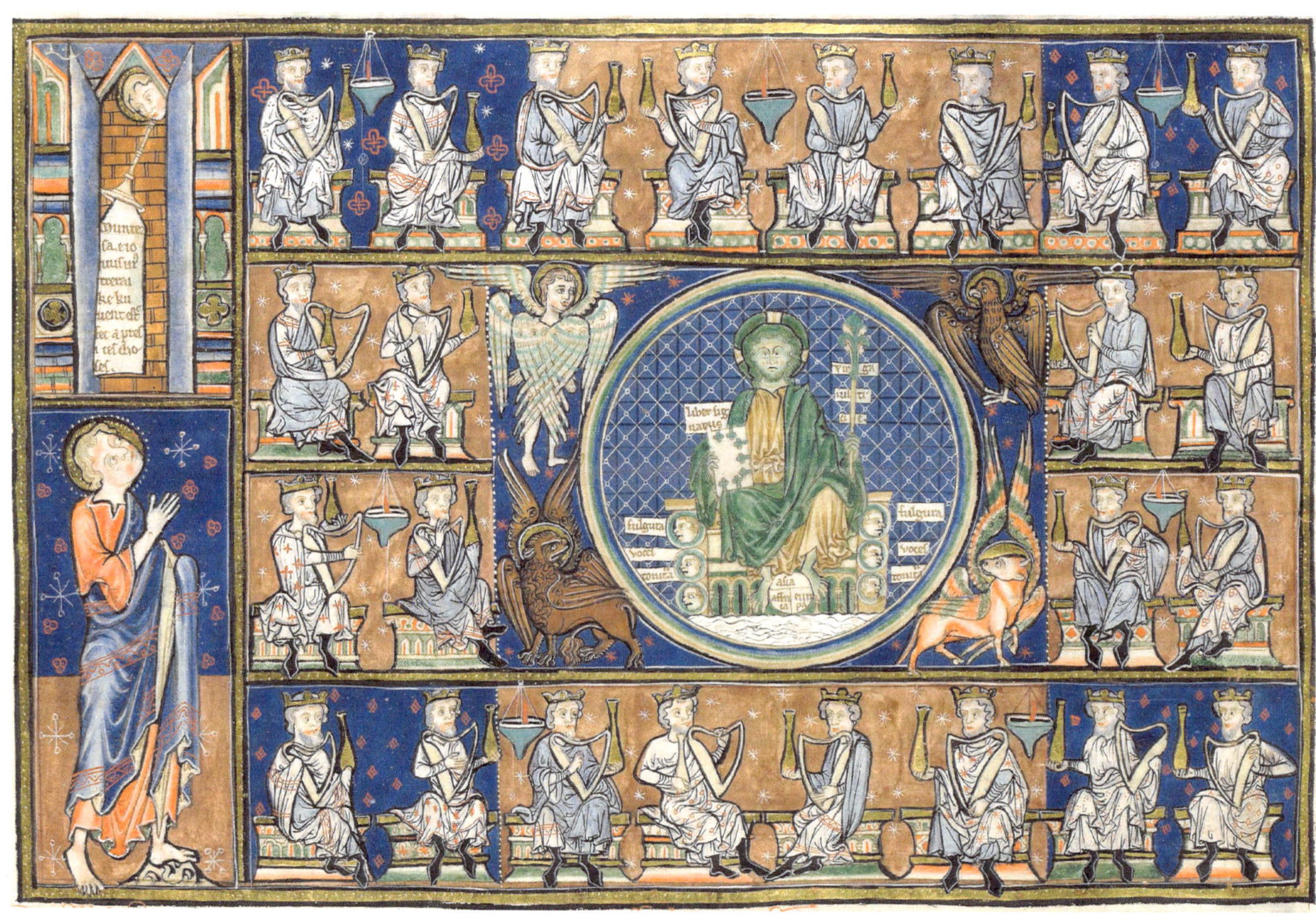

the voice addressing John and imply it is the same voice as the one recorded in the first vision, alerting us to the fact that the visions in Revelation may be connected in more than one way.

The circular "bow" I have painted as a rainbow, the most likely interpretation. It becomes an open door into heaven and reminds me of the words in a hymn by William Cowper: "Sometimes a light surprises the Christian while he sings ..." "Heaven" is closer to earth than we think. In the midst of worshipping God, for example, we too may see the light of heaven and have our eyes momentarily opened by His Spirit.

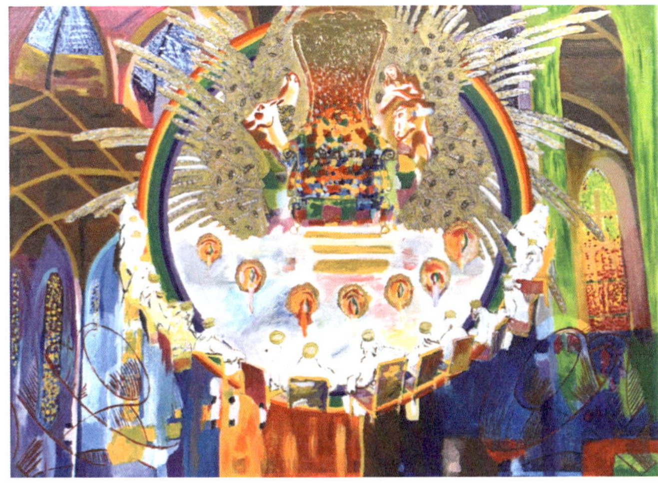

The precious stones mentioned indicate a very bright, colourful place: the light emanating from the throne is reflected and refracted in a bright interplay. I find it extraordinary that the illuminators of old have not represented this in their paintings.

Another twenty-four thrones are mentioned. Seated on them are elders, dressed in white and bearing golden crowns. Is it the "control centre" of all rule and authority that John is being shown here? A council of power over the world?

Who are these "elders", and who do they represent/rule? We are not told! Some suggest angels, glorified people or other heavenly beings. The vision makes clear that they are important, for they are mentioned first. There are visual links to some of the promises made to the churches in Revelation 3 – the conqueror's crown, the white robe ... The number 24 suggests they are representatives of God's people, according to Koester. [Later in 5:8 they are shown to be involved in the prayers of the saints. So there seems to be a connection, but it is not fully spelled out.] Leithart thinks they are connected with the OT saints, and he sees them "disappear as Revelation moves to its conclusion, replaced by victorious martyrs".

Why do lightning and thunder and voices emanate from the throne? Bauckham rightly suggests the lightning, thunder and voices indicate a manifestation of God's holiness, emphasized by the fact that God cannot be seen in this vision. [We will see lightning, thunder and voices amplified three more times, at the opening of the seventh seal in 8:5, the seventh trumpet in 11:19 and the seventh bowl in 16:18–21. This amplification reveals God's judgement on all evil; it also highlights why we should read Revelation in sequence, from beginning to end.] I have depicted thunder and lightning with trumpets (in the lower corners) and the flashing wings of the living creatures (in the upper half). In Medieval paintings they were usually located under the seat of the throne: three heads protruding on each side, as you can see in the *Trinity* image on the left page.

What are the seven torches? The Bible tells us they refer to "the seven spirits of God", or the seven-fold spirit of God (see 1:4; 3:1), a clear reference to the work and ministry of the Holy Spirit.

What is the crystal sea, and what does it represent? Scholars connect it to the "sea" in front of the Jerusalem temple. Caird shows it to be the "remnant" of evil in heaven. I find that idea attractive but problematical. John describes what he sees as "like a sea", and it has the appearance of "glass-like crystal". Most of the illuminators have not included this in their illustration. Perhaps this "sea" in heaven is more a reminder of the cleansing required by the purity of heaven?

Let's stop for a moment to reflect on the wonder of John seeing the unseeable, and writing down what cannot be comprehended in words. He saw into heaven, not God's face but God revealing Himself in glory. He sees and experiences how God is worshipped by those surrounding the throne. John sees and writes down what he sees as best he can, being reminded of Ezekiel's and Isaiah's visions of heaven. Those descriptions are quite different. And John does not try to edit what he sees to match the earlier visions. We learn from each vision in its own terms how to worship God aright.

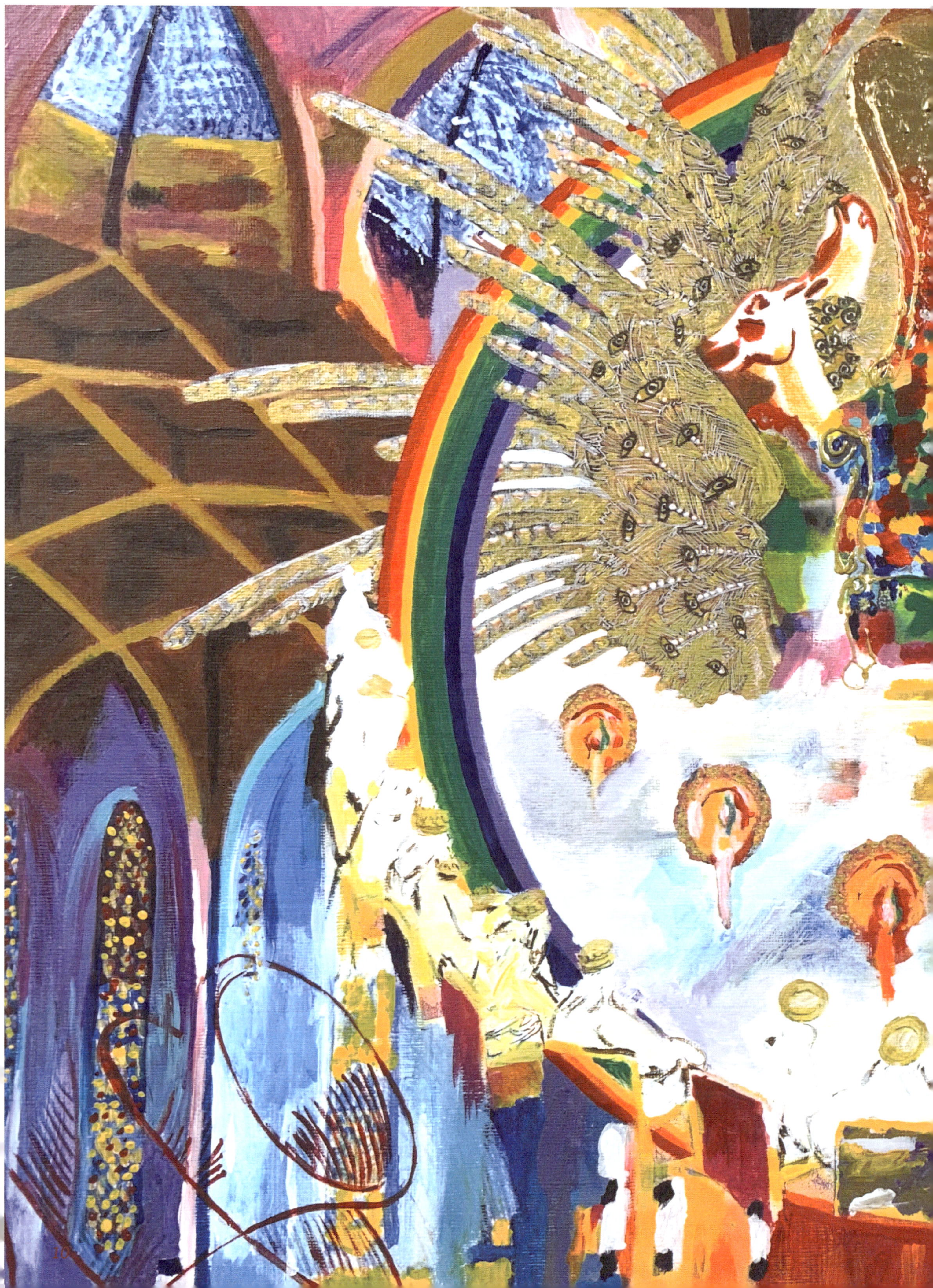

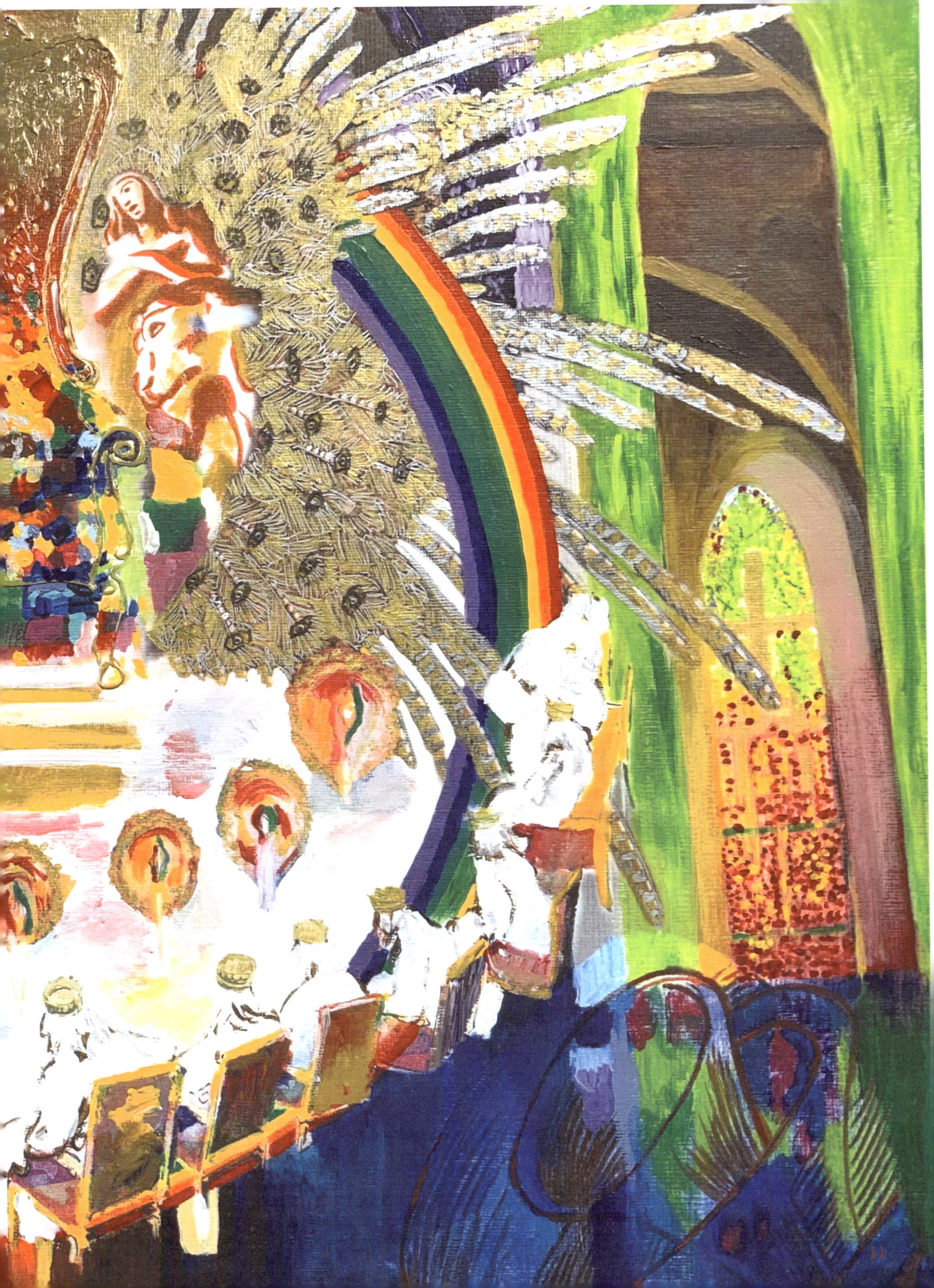

Precious Stones (Detail)

In this Story I will focus on just four precious stones: *iaspis, sardius, smaragdos* and *crystallos*. [In Rev 21 I will refer to all twelve, as they also feature in the new Jerusalem.] When you compare different Bible translations, you will quickly note that the lists of stones in Revelation are not always translated the same way. And commentators seem very unsure what these stones are/were.

> *4: [3]And the one seated there looks like jasper and carnelian, and around the throne is a rainbow that looks like an emerald ...*
> *[6]and in front of the throne there is something like a sea of glass, like crystal.*

Take *iaspis*. It is very often translated as "jasper" – except for *The Jewish Bible*, which translates it as "diamond", as does the Dutch Bible translation of 1954 (NBG). But what did *iaspis* mean to the first readers, and can we use that to figure out what it means today? A name could refer to a single stone or to a group (or family) of stones. Also, some precious stones we know today were not available at all or known in earlier times.

Iaspis is a Greek word, used also in the Greek translation of the OT (the Septuagint) to translate a Hebrew term. Theologians and geologists have joined forces to try and determine what stone it describes.

In early times, precious stones were identified by their colour. But today we identify them by their chemical structure, hardness and lustre. Jasper, for example, was found in many colours. Theologians of the past often chose green as its most likely colour, and so they elaborated on the possible symbolic meanings of green in the context of Revelation. *Iaspis* also appears in the OT on the breastplate of the high priest. There, however, it is not described as being so exceptionally different from the other stones as *iaspis* appears to be in Revelation 4 and 21. It is the comparison of the stones in Revelation 21 and the stones of the breastplate that has complicated this study of stones in our text. Especially the way the Septuagint translated the Hebrew names adds a layer of complexity.

Bolman, a Dutch geologist and theologian, concluded that *iaspis* in the OT was what we now know as "jasper"; but that in the NT it should be translated as "diamond", a jewel which was not known to the Israelites in the desert nor obtained from Egypt. But diamond was found in India and imported into the Roman Empire from the start of the first century. Bolman's work has never been translated into English and is not quoted by English-speaking geologists or theologians, although the Dutch Bible Society in 1954 was convinced by his argument in their new Bible translation. The following is a translated summary of the main sources Bolman uses to support his argument:

Dionysius, Perieg, (AD 117–138), V.780 writes: "Near the banks of Thermodon [river in Turkey ending the Black Sea] you will find the water coloured *iaspis*." And in V.724: "You will find the heavenly blue *iaspis* near the Caspian Sea." And in V.1114: "In India people seek for the green-shining *iaspis*."

Dioscorides, AD 60, in m.m.5.159 tells us that the *iaspis* looks "sometimes like a *smaragdion*, sometimes like a *krustallion*".

Plinius (AD 77), Hist.Nat 37.8.37: "The *iaspis* is green, mainly transparent, also blue, purple, cloudy coloured, violet, rose red, pistachio green, and other colours. Mainly used as *sphragis* (seals)."

With this, Bolman shows that *iaspis* was a collective name, rather than a word for one particular stone, and that transparency was what all *iaspis* had in common. The most valuable ones were uncoloured, water-clear. Likely candidates include diamond, rock crystal, white zircon, white beryl, white corundum. In the first century, *adamas* (=diamond) was also a collective name (Plinius, Hist.Nat. 37.4.15). According to Bolman *adamas* was included under the older collective name *iaspis*, which originated in the Hellenistic period and was used by the Romans; *adamas* was originally used for hardened steel and only later on (as the character of the stone became better known?) was applied to diamonds ...

Bolman's theological case rests on the fact that *iaspis* is described as "transparent" in Revelation 21, and that this stone had to be the most valuable and most exquisite! After having read many historical sources and journal articles written over the last 150 years, and many commentaries, I became convinced by Bolman's arguments that in Revelation, *iaspis* is best translated as "diamond".

What is the colour of *iaspis*? I portray diamond as multi-coloured, and I paint it in a stylized way reminiscent of the modern work of Mondrian. I was thrilled to discover that diamond has a basic cubic structure, in line with the (perfect) cubic shape of both the Holy of Holies in the Jerusalem temple and the new Jerusalem in Revelation! And multi-colour seems to be the most appropriate colour to associate with our God: especially as the "addition" of all the colours (in light) yields perfect white!

Of the other stones mentioned in Revelation 3, *sardius* is easier to identify. It refers to a red stone, either carnelian or the darker sards we know. Some translations have ruby, but there seems to be a scholarly consensus that this cannot be. [I will return to this in Rev 21.]

For *smaragdos* most scholars see a green/turquoise emerald, though to imagine it as a green rainbow is a challenge. I responded with a double layer of green in the circular rainbow. More than a century ago, Flinders Petrie identified this stone as "rock crystal". He could not conceive of a green rainbow and suggested rock crystal is known to refract the rainbow perfectly. Cooper dismissed this in 1945 saying a fault in the stone causes that phenomenon. The theologian Swete also discounted the argument as he did not think the description dealt with a rainbow at all, but just a "bow". In his defense, Petrie quoted the fact that Nero had a pair of spectacles made of *smaragdos*, which would surely exclude our emerald. I feel Petrie may be closest to the truth. And rock crystal is colourless but brilliant at reflecting light in multiple rainbows!

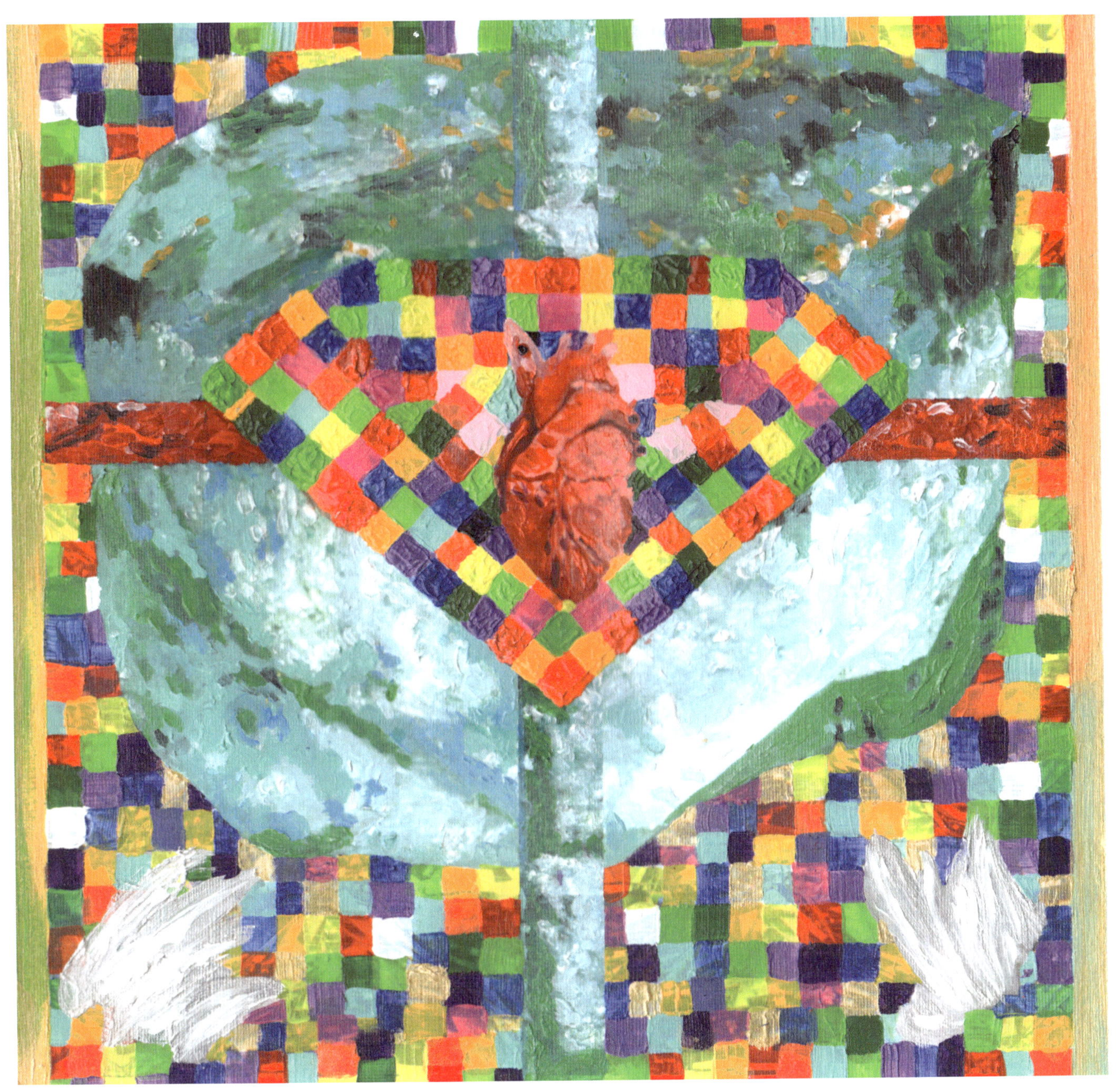

Does it matter what the stones or colours are? Most theologians do not delve into these specifics (and you will now appreciate why). Sometimes they comment with a commonplace like "God shines like and is costlier than any jewel", but such glib conclusions fail to address why John recorded the stones with such detailed descriptions. [I will return to this discussion again in Rev 21.] For now, jewels are special, precious and diverse, and God has chosen to use them to depict Himself and His people. God is light. The future is bright! The distinct splendour with which His creation and His people reflect His glory, matters to God. It is not "accidental"; it is intentional. Each reflects with an own special and distinct glory the light of the one who is light. God notices that. So, should we not also take note?

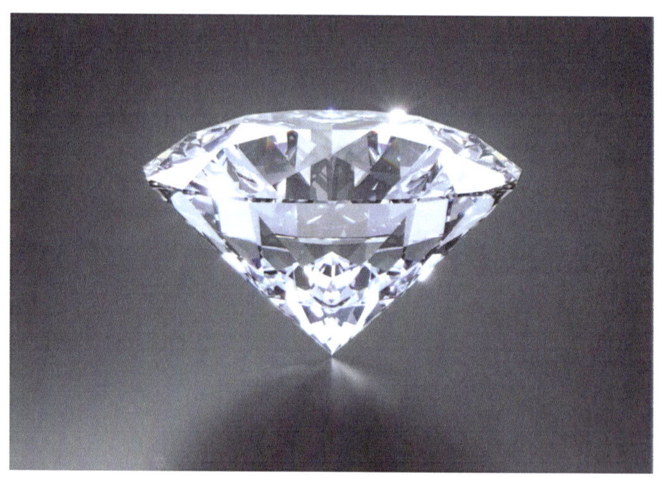

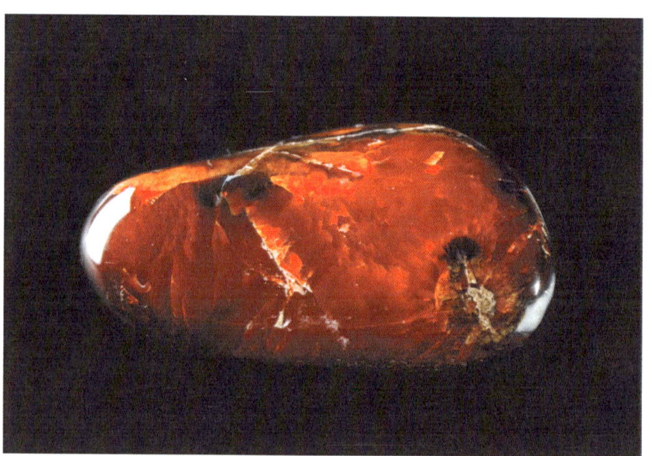

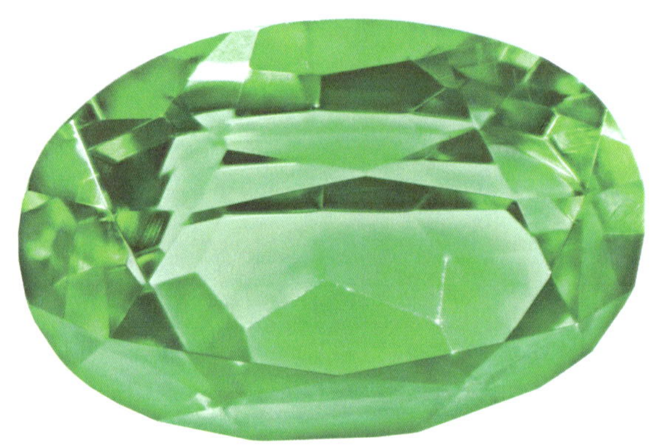

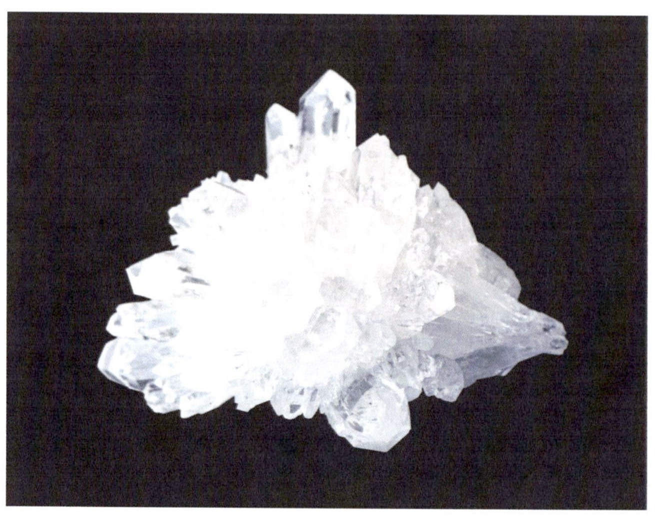

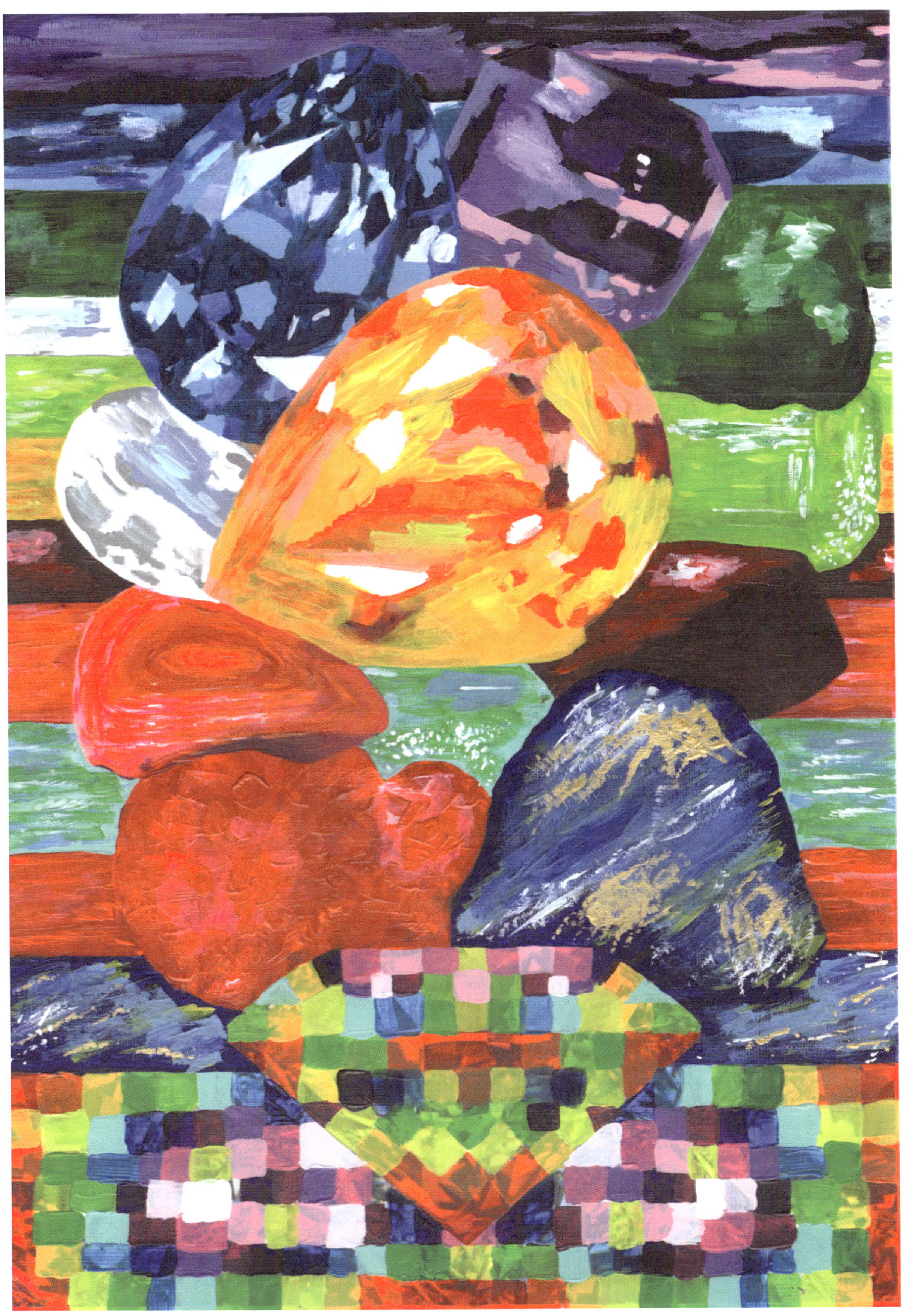

Holy, Holy, Holy

Who are the four living creatures? The "living creatures" are angelic beings who seem to have a life and identity of their own, related to the cherubim and the seraphim of the OT. It is generally agreed that they are connected to God and His creation to represent God in an executive way. [They also become the executors of judgement in 15:7.] They are primarily linked with the throne of God; so I have painted them very closely connected to the throne, as in Ezekiel's vision. My main inspiration here are the lithographs of Hans Feibusch in *The Revelation of St John the Divine* and I have directly quoted his "creatures" in my painting. It is best to think of these creatures as connected with creation in a similar way as elders are connected with the people of God. Here God is interested in his whole creation, not just people.

Why a flying eagle? One creature is described in movement; the others are stagnant. I wonder why that is, as all the creatures have six wings. Perhaps because it is "in flight" that the eagle shows its strength, or particularly reflects God's glory?

Next we, the readers, follow John as he enters the liturgy, for the elders and creatures are in heavenly worship. And, as we shall find out [in, for example Rev 5:7], what happens in heavenly worship has direct relevance to earth, creation, and the church, God's people.

4: 6 *Around the throne, and on each side of the throne, are four living creatures, full of eyes in front and behind:* 7 *the first living creature like a lion, the second living creature like an ox, the third living creature with a face like a human face, and the fourth living creature like a flying eagle.* 8 *And the four living creatures, each of them with six wings, are full of eyes all around and inside. Day and night without ceasing they sing, "Holy, holy, holy, the Lord God the Almighty, who was and is and is to come."* 9 *And whenever the living creatures give glory and honor and thanks to the one who is seated on the throne, who lives forever and ever,* 10 *the twenty-four elders fall before the one who is seated on the throne and worship the one who lives forever and ever; they cast their crowns before the throne, singing,* 11 *"You are worthy, our Lord and God, to receive glory and honor and power, for you created all things, and by your will they existed and were created."*

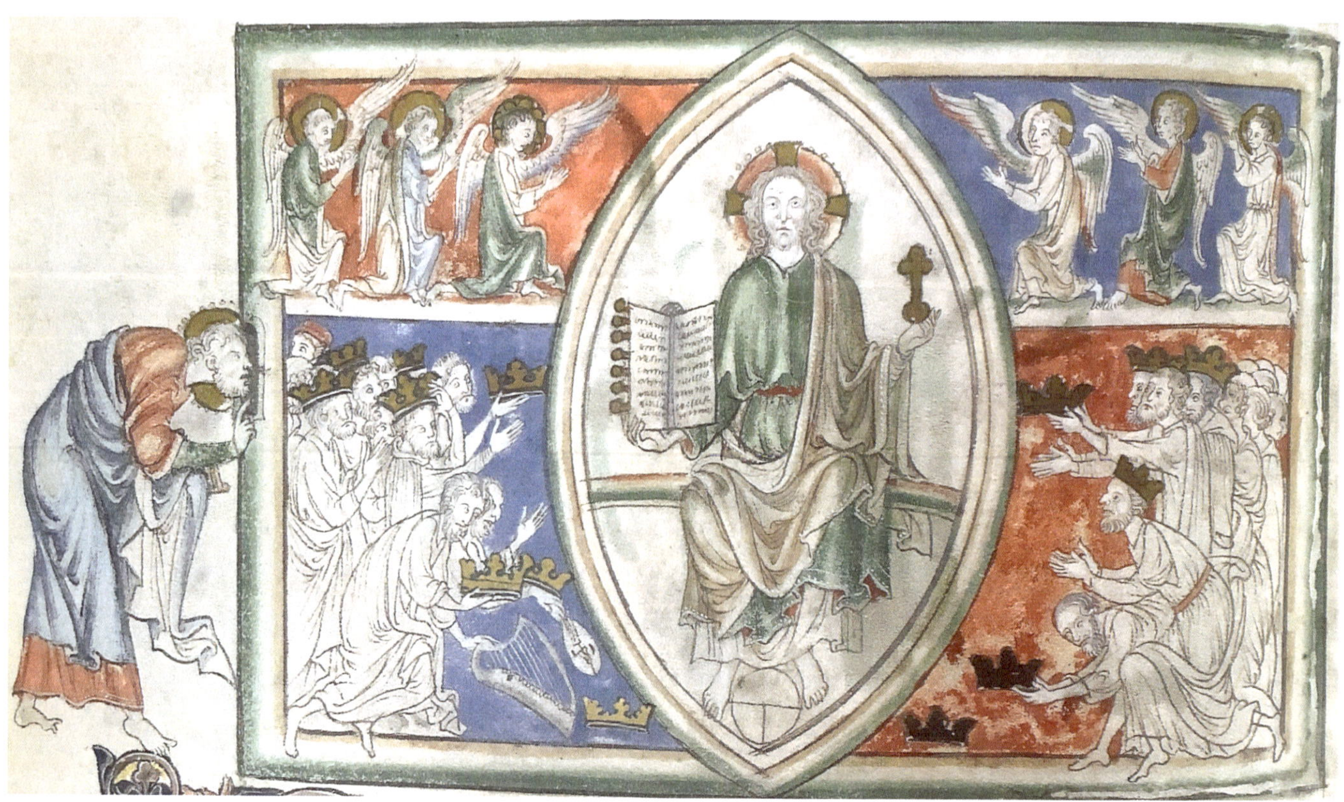

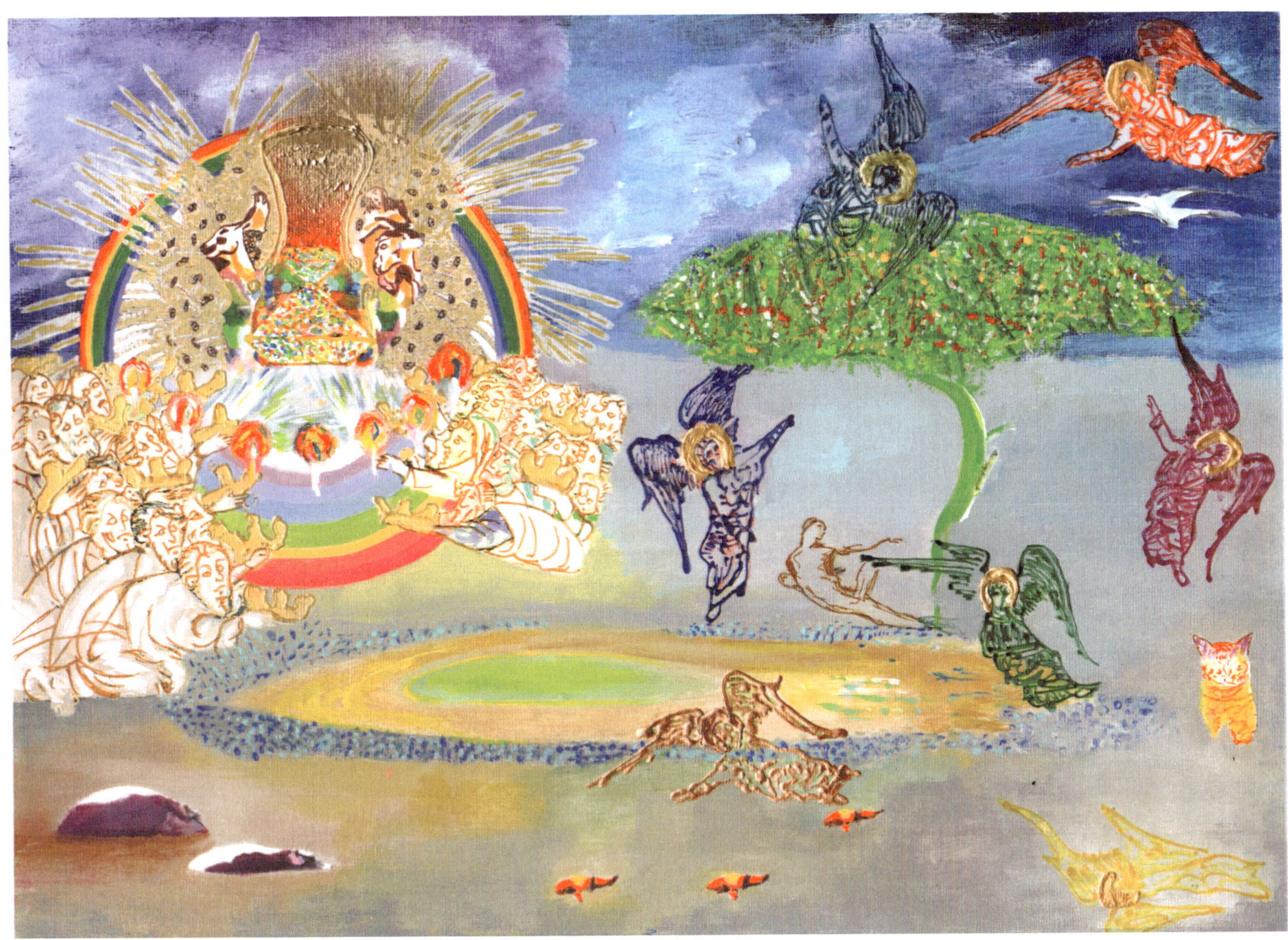

There is clearly a difference between the songs in Revelation 4 and 5. In Revelation 4, creation and the coming of God is in view; in Revelation 5 it is the new creation and Jesus [and in Rev 7, the innumerable people of God].

Finally, I should mention that the opening verse in this chapter is often used to insert a very long period of time, during which allegedly a "rapture" of the church takes place. There is no direct mention of such an event in the text. The word "after" here should be understood like the time verses in 1:3, simply indicating this vision follows the previous one. The "future" in the text refers to the future of the first readers. I can see no basis in the text for unnaturally lengthening the period.

What to do? "Worship God and Him only"! "Let us therefore approach the throne of grace with boldness, so that we may receive mercy and find grace to help in time of need" (Heb 4:16).

I rather like the way John peeps into the scene of heaven in the *Getty* illustration, but John had been called into heaven himself!

I have concentrated on the whole of creation in my image. The elders and the living creatures worship the Seated one. I painted the tree of life surrounded by the *Beatus* septet of angels. I quote the Adam from Michelangelo and added some of my favourite creatures: hippos from Kenya, fish from South Africa, birds from New Zealand, our cat Tigger, much loved by all who lived and worked in our house in Carlisle, and an African lizard. The "creation pool" was photographed in Rotorua, New Zealand, where creation still appears to be taking place.

Let all creation worship Him, who is seated on the throne. Hallelujah!

John in Tears

Anneke Kaai's painting concentrates attention on the scroll. I love her work for its clear portrayal of the "handover" as John weeps, then dries his tears when the elder comforts him with the revelation of Jesus Christ. The lion, with the lamb as teeth, seems a wonderful visual solution to one of the central themes of the book of Revelation.

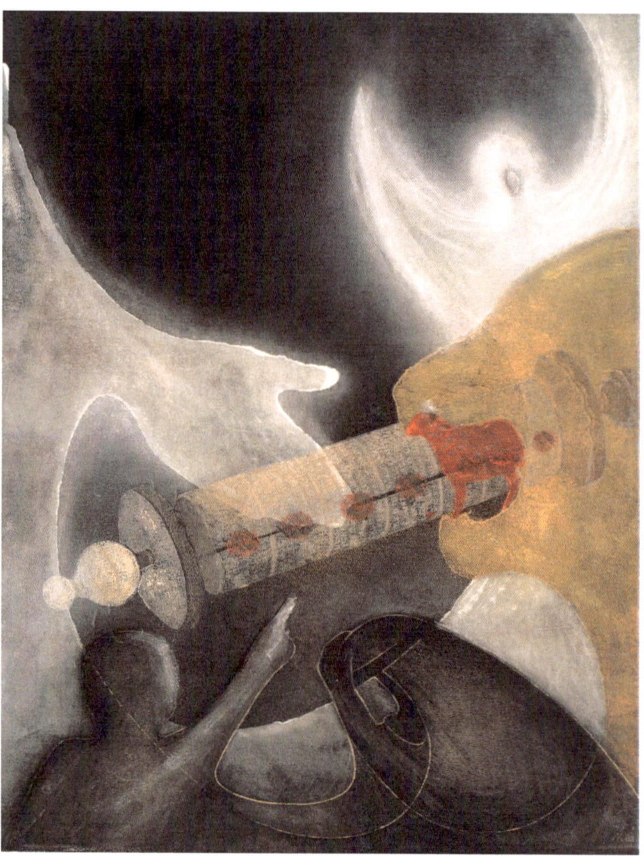

In my painting I have concentrated on the tears of John. I quote John from the bust of the 500 BC philosopher Heraclitus of Ephesus, "a melancholic, self-taught pioneer of wisdom". The angel announces the scroll. The hand of God holds it out, showing seven (real) wax seals. I designed their stamp to be the "tree of life" I photographed in the Masai Mara.

What does it mean for the scroll to be written on the inside and on the back? A number of solutions have been suggested. Zahn argues that Origen got it wrong (and with him most of the modern translations that followed him when he suggested the scroll was written on both sides, quoting Ezek 2:10). In Ezekiel, the scroll is not sealed. Why seal a scroll so securely if anyone can read the outside, Zahn asks. He argues the Greek

> *5: [1]Then I saw in the right hand of the one seated on the throne a scroll written on the inside and on the back, sealed with seven seals; [2]and I saw a mighty angel proclaiming with a loud voice, "Who is worthy to open the scroll and break its seals?" [3]And no one in heaven or on earth or under the earth was able to open the scroll or to look into it. [4]And I began to weep bitterly because no one was found worthy to open the scroll or to look into it. [5]Then one of the elders said to me, "Do not weep. See, the Lion of the tribe of Judah, the Root of David, has conquered, so that he can open the scroll and its seven seals."*

text suggests it is written on the inside and sealed on the outside with seven seals. That makes sense to me.

What is the content of this scroll? This is not spelled out by John. Which has not stopped commentators from making many suggestions. Boxall, for example, helpfully suggests that God's right hand connoted power to bring judgement and salvation (Exod 15:6; Ps 48:10; Isa 41:10), so his holding the scroll in his right hand suggests that its contents involve both of those aspects of God's work. Other suggestions include the book of Life, God's plan for the world, the Bible, both OT and NT. Koester has a helpful summary. To me, the best suggestion seems that they are the visions later seen in the Book of Revelation, probably starting with the trumpets, but we will get greater clarity as we read on and the seals have all been opened.

Why the tears of John? No one was found to be able to open the scroll. John gets very emotional and cries in disappointment. He has been called into this vision (4:1) to be shown "what must take place after this". If no one worthy is found, would God's purpose then be thwarted? Is it because John senses that this revelation is a matter of life and death that he is so overcome with sadness at his utter helplessness in the situation? John is not a cool objective observer ... He is drawn into the vision with body and soul, with tears and despair ... We do well to open our own hearts as we read this, to feel tears burning as we read on ...

But the elders have "inside" knowledge. One tells John there is a worthy one: the Lion of the tribe of Judah and the Root of David. Yes, he is talking of Jesus the Messiah, Jesus the King. We come across this designation again and again: Jesus, the Lion from the tribe of Judah, the Messiah who fulfils the first covenant, the "old" song. John may have felt encouraged at this point to expect an impressive royal entrance.

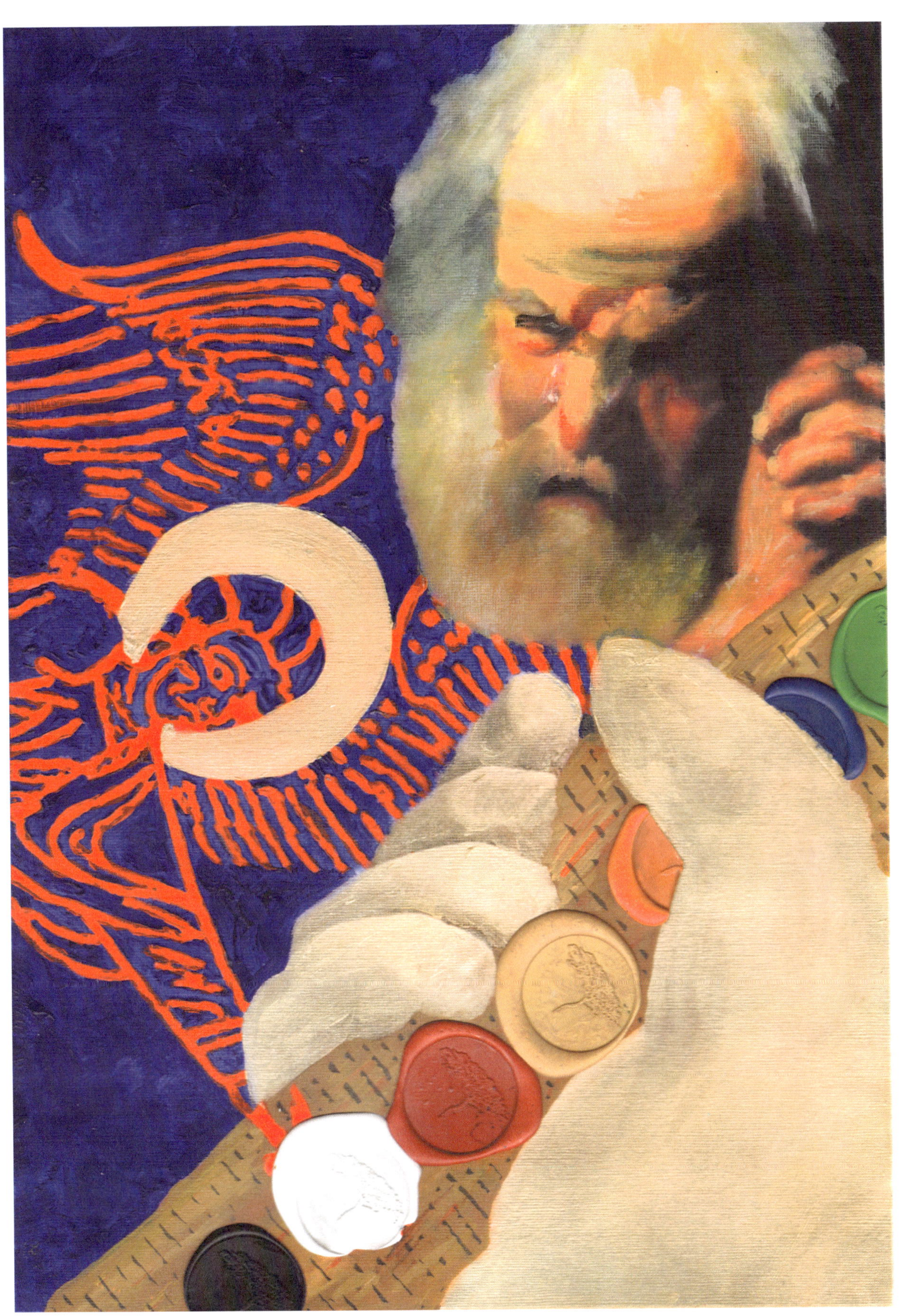

The Lamb

We heard about the Lion of Judah and the Root of David, but what John sees between the throne and the four creatures, and among the elders, is a Lamb, looking as if slaughtered, with seven horns and seven eyes.

In my painting I have used the Dwennimmen, one of the Ghanian Adinkra symbols: seven ram's horns, indicating humility and strength. The colours are those of the jewels on and around the throne. The four living creatures and the elders are watching the Lamb. I quoted the Lamb from the Ghent altarpiece, one of the most well-known depictions of the Lamb in the history of western art.

The *Getty* illustration portrays the Lamb more literally, with seven eyes and seven horns, on top of an altar. John is shown on his knees, eagerly looking in on the scene, not missing any detail.

Why seven horns? They indicate full and total strength.

> 5: [6]*Then I saw between the throne and the four living creatures and among the elders a Lamb standing as if it had been slaughtered, having seven horns and seven eyes, which are the seven spirits of God sent out into all the earth.* [7]*He went and took the scroll from the right hand of the one who was seated on the throne.*

Why seven eyes? The seven eyes scan everything. They are the seven spirits sent out into all the earth, referring to the Holy Spirit (see also Story Twelve). As the lamb has only two eyes here,[1] my painting alludes to five more.

Why a lion and a lamb, are they not contradictory metaphors? The slaughtered Lamb fulfils the OT in weakness, not in strength, in sacrifice and self-giving. The lion is a lion with lamb's teeth. We too only conquer in weakness and sacrifice. I advise all readers to read Bauckham for a full exposition of this chapter (see *The Theology of the Book of Revelation*).

1. Restoration of this work in 2019 surprisingly revealed "humanoid", full frontal eyes. As reported by the BBC, 22/1/20.

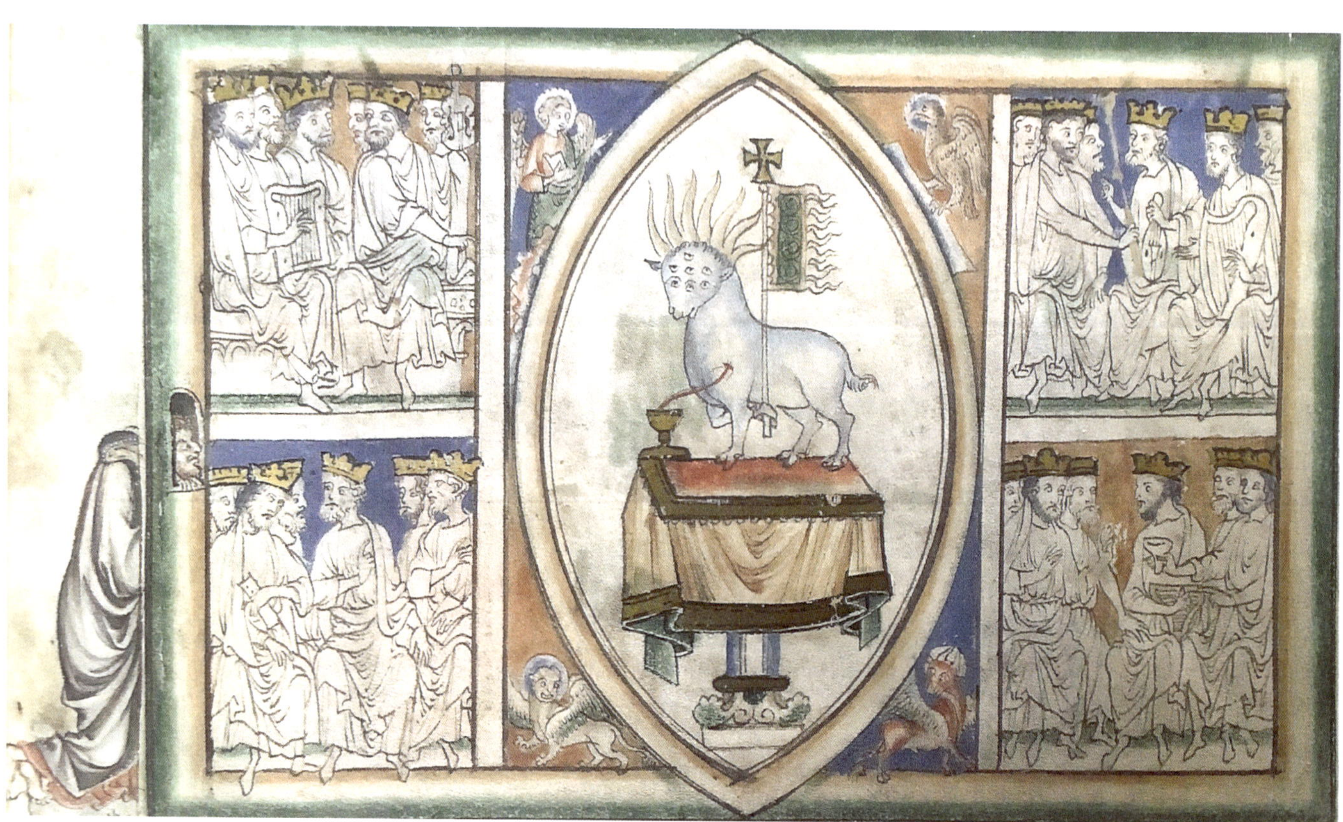

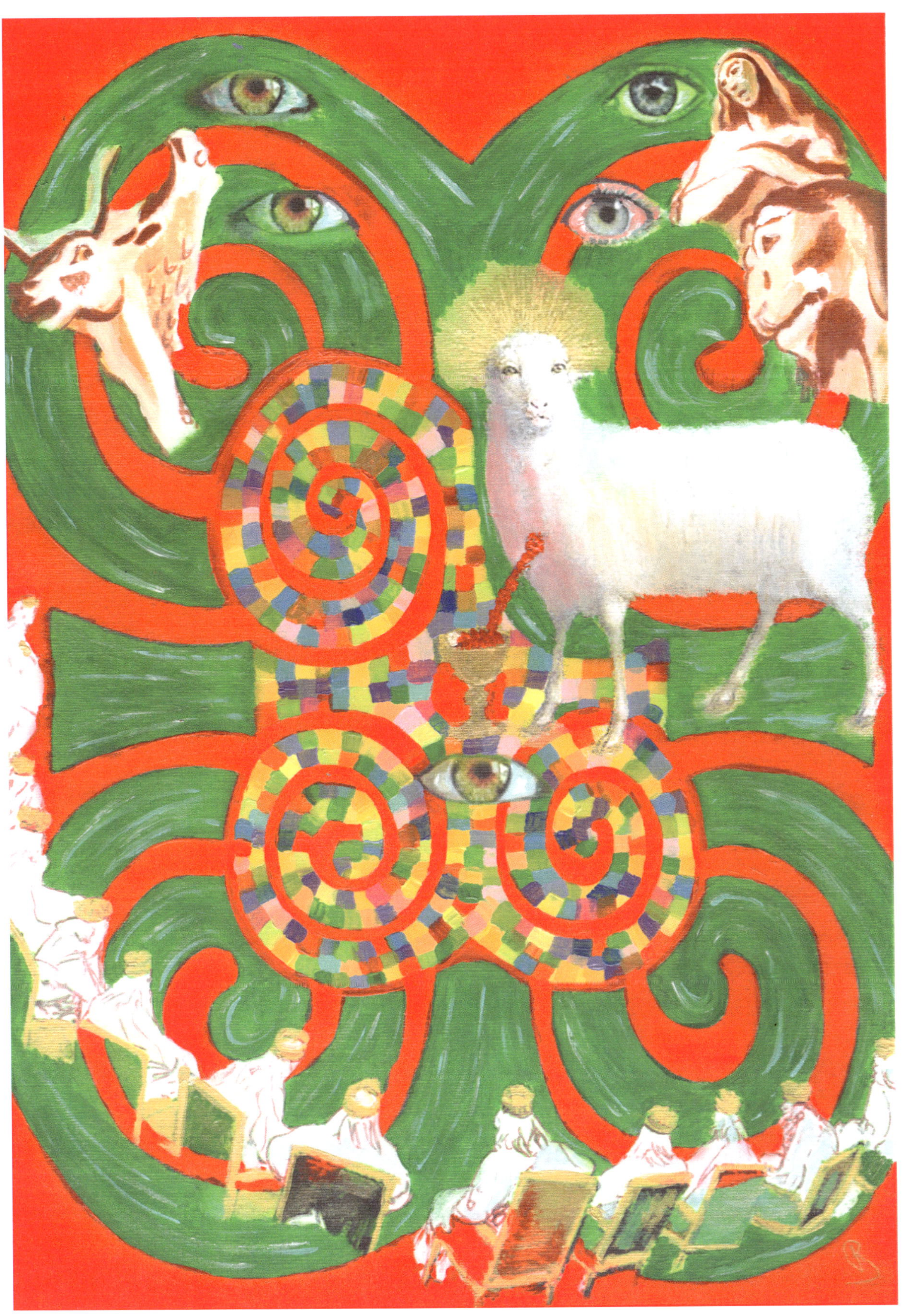

A New Song

The Lamb with the scroll is the focus here of the living creatures and elders, who with harps and the prayers of the saints worship Him in a brand-new song.

In the *Beatus* image below, you can see the angels in all their glory. I have quoted, and will quote them throughout this project. I do love this particular *Beatus* painting with the Lamb in the centre, under the throne of the Seated one and surrounded by the living creatures and elders. The living creatures on their wheels refer to Ezekiel 1.

My own painting is very different. I wanted to visualize the new song with lots of violins, a harp and "dancing" angels (designed and drawn by my granddaughter Zahra, my eager assistant and, at times, teacher). Here the angels of *Beatus* become part of the worship celebration, abandoning their "holding up the world". The elders are quoted from the *1313*.

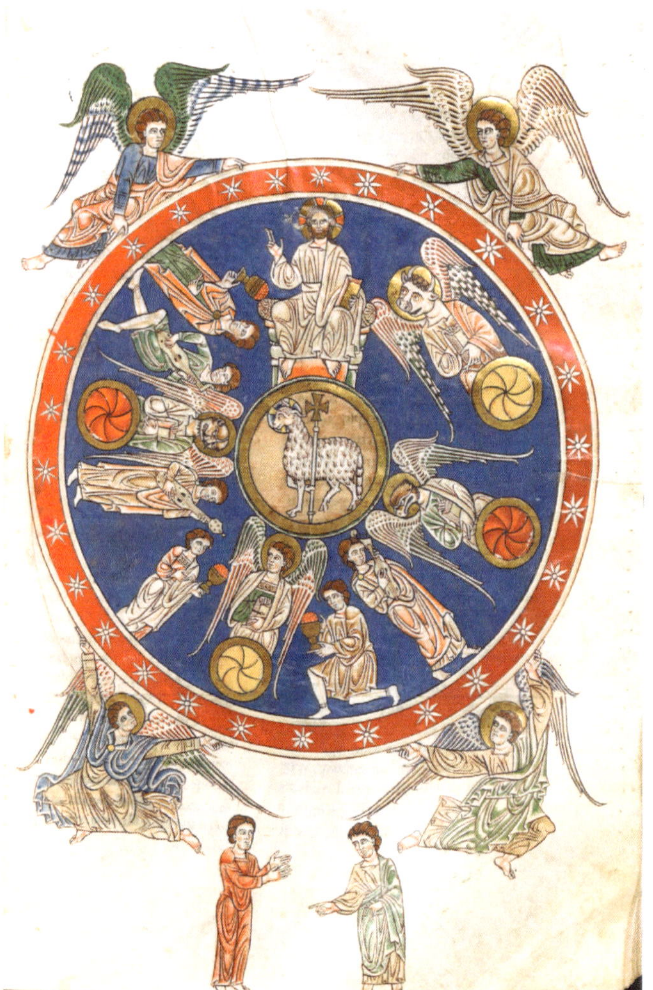

5: [8]When he had taken the scroll, the four living creatures and the twenty-four elders fell before the Lamb, each holding a harp and golden bowls full of incense, which are the prayers of the saints. [9]They sing a new song: "You are worthy to take the scroll and to open its seals, for you were slaughtered and by your blood you ransomed for God saints from every tribe and language and people and nation; [10]you have made them to be a kingdom and priests serving our God, and they will reign on earth." [11]Then I looked, and I heard the voice of many angels surrounding the throne and the living creatures and the elders; they numbered myriads of myriads and thousands of thousands, [12]singing with full voice, "Worthy is the Lamb that was slaughtered to receive power and wealth and wisdom and might and honor and glory and blessing!" [13]Then I heard every creature in heaven and on earth and under the earth and in the sea, and all that is in them, singing, "To the one seated on the throne and to the Lamb be blessing and honor and glory and might forever and ever!" [14]And the four living creatures said, "Amen!" And the elders fell down and worshiped.

The Lamb-as-if-slaughtered is again quoted from Van Eyck. All – in heaven, on earth, under the earth and in the sea, hence the layers and the creatures (including a handsome chameleon by my grandson Lucas) – are worshipping the Lamb. I have chosen joyful pink as the main colour, a combination of red (suffering) and white (purity). The incense (the prayers of the saints) also adds to this explosion of joy that surrounds the Lamb, who has been revealed as worthy! Amen. Let us worship Him with child-like extravagance, alongside all of creation.

What is this "new" song? The first thing to notice is that it is actually being sung! Previously the worshippers speak (*legontes*), but here for the first time they also sing (*adousin*). And the song is linked to bowls of incense, the prayers of the saints. Most importantly, the new song is for the new myriads of "saints", from every tribe and people and language and nation, not only from one chosen group. They are the new kings and priests, and their new song has a surprising new subject: the Lamb-as-if-slaughtered.

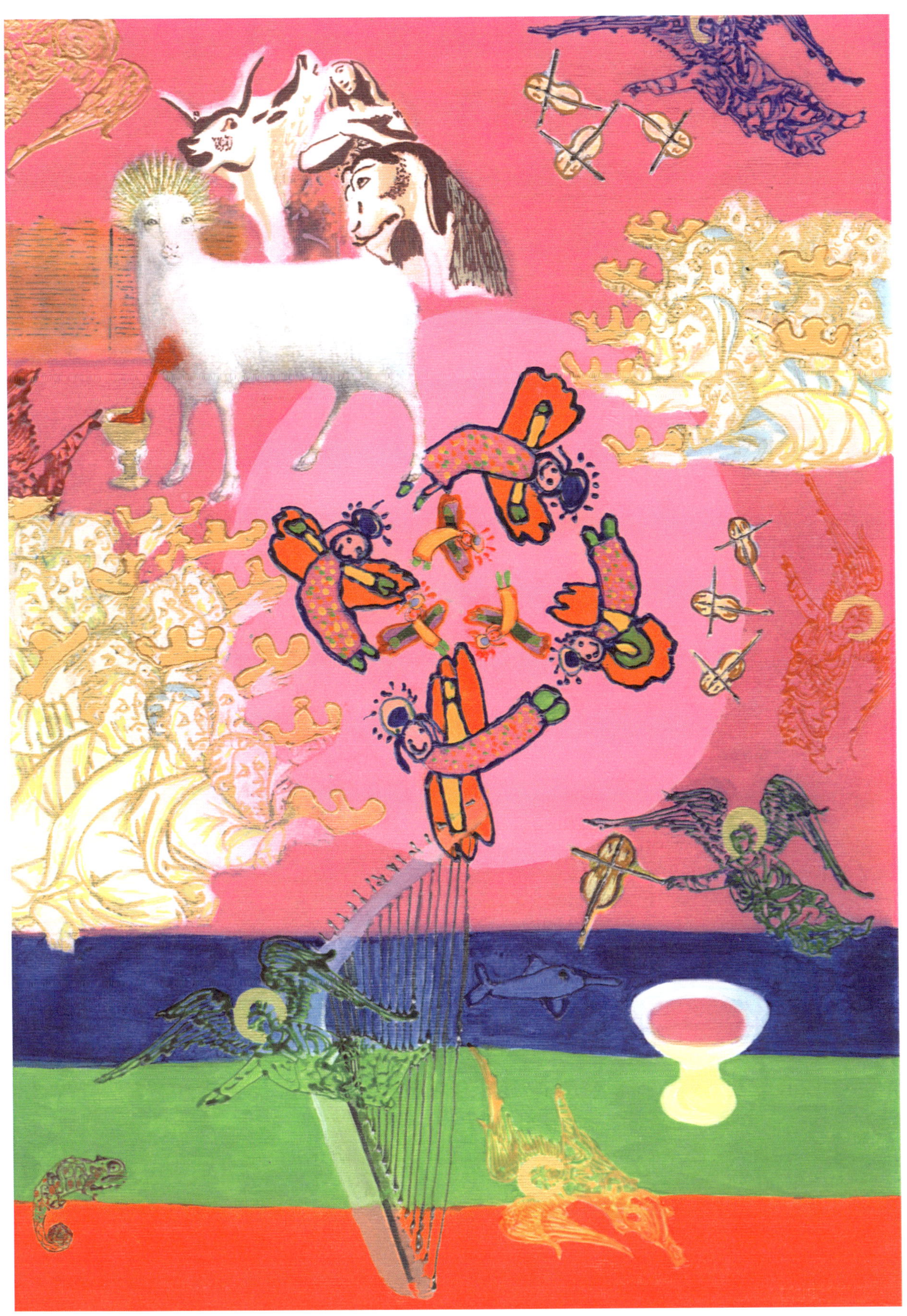

Visual Meditation 1

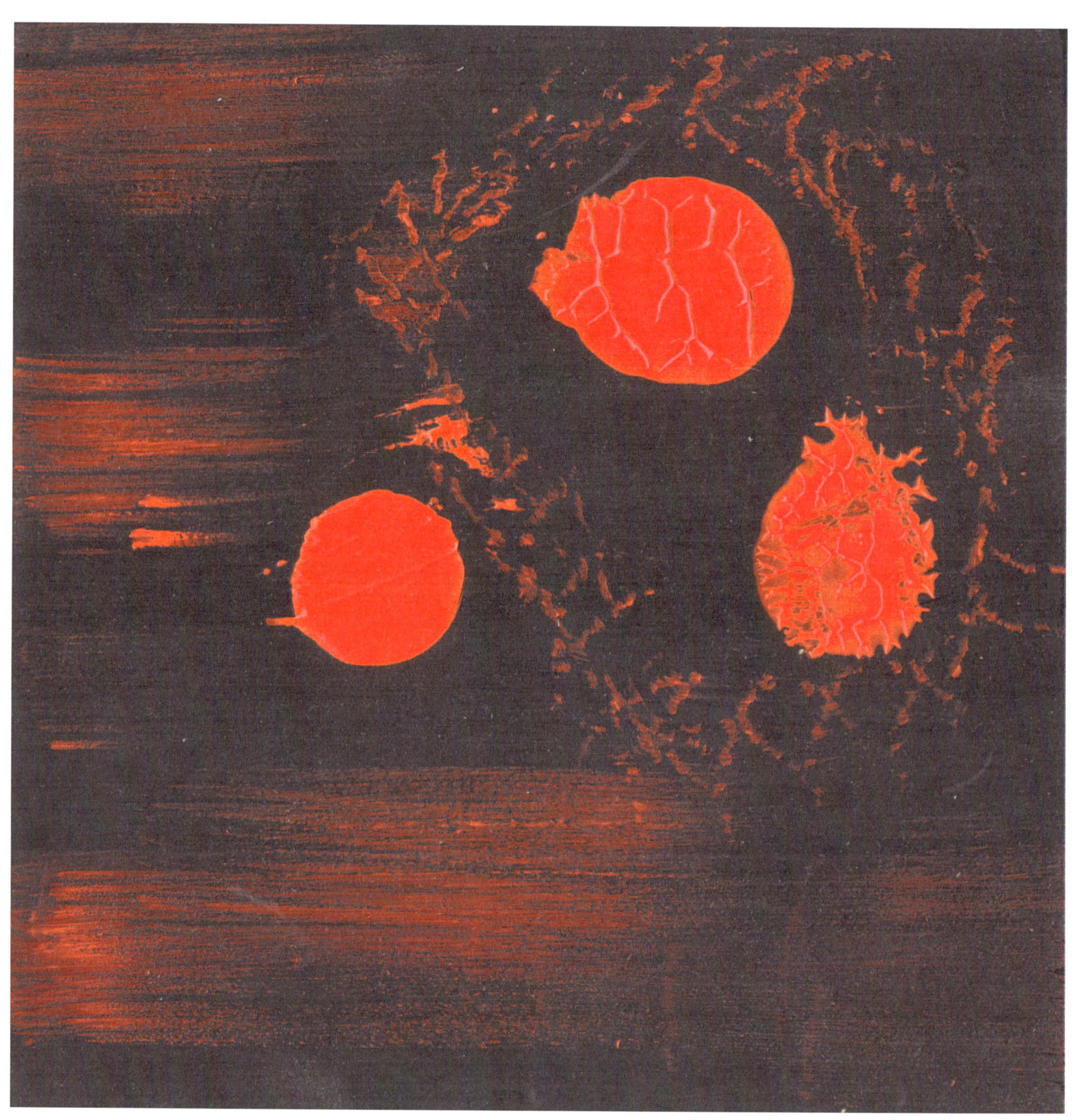

Bloody crown

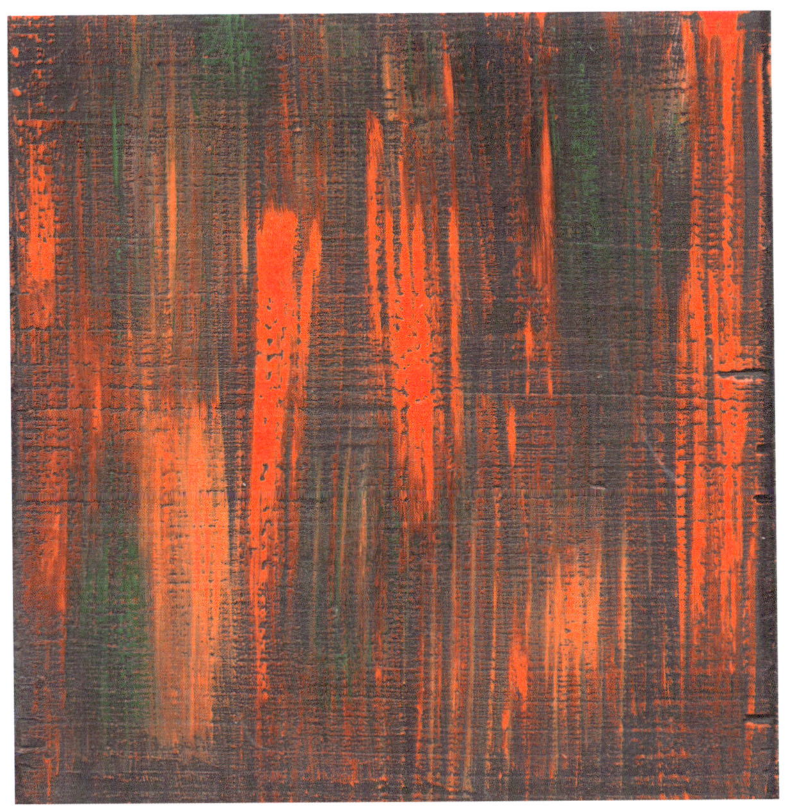

Blood redeeming

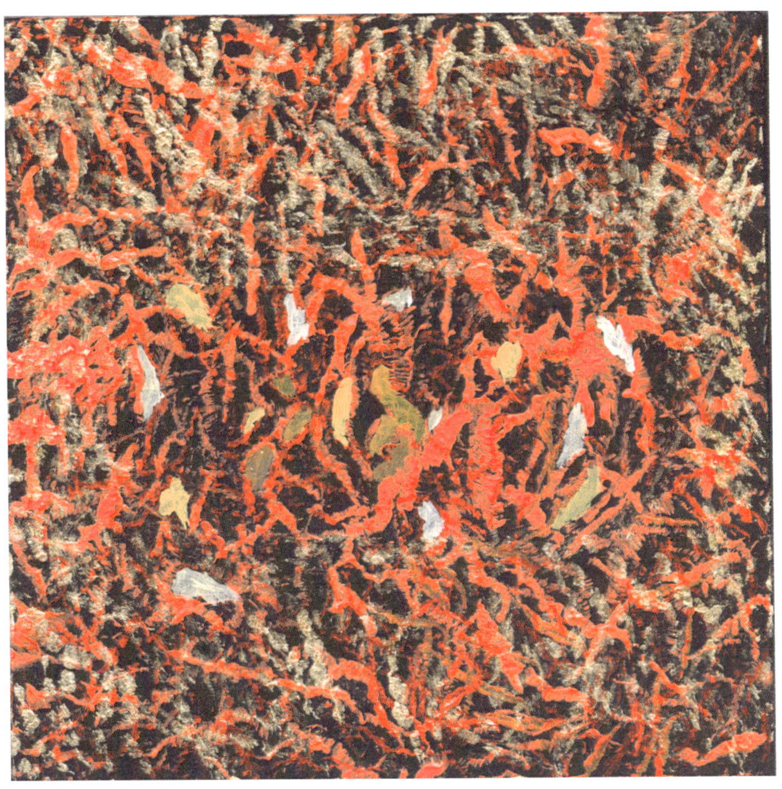

Pentecost

Four Horsemen

We now come to the well-known "four horsemen of the apocalypse". Dürer's masterly executed woodcut has become their iconic image. Next to it, below, is the *Beatus* image. I like the colour of *Beatus* and find it closer to the meaning of the text than Dürer is. The *Apokalipsis in Dietsche* (a Flemish MS from AD 1400) is closer still. It gives a good portrayal in stunning colour of all the horses, in context after the opening of all the seals. I have quoted the horses from this work (on the page to the right) in my paintings on the first four unsealings.

I have resisted painting all four horses together, seeing this has been done so many times and gives, I believe, the wrong impression. Many modern scholars commend Dürer for his placing the horses at equal level in a mission of terror and judgement. But, as I will show, I believe the first horse is separate from the others. And the history of interpretation is on my side in this.

Are these real horses? They come from heaven and go to earth at the command of the living creatures. They are not real or literal. But, as we shall see, they represent various powers unleashed under the careful eye of the Lamb. Their purpose is to unveil Christ, past present and future, and show us what we need to do.

What do the riders represent? This is very much debated. Only the fourth one is named: Death. The others are not, but if one has been personalized perhaps the others can be too. Some have suggested they are all evil. Others, that they all represent Christ. And still others suggest the first one is Christ, but the other three are evil. What did strike me is how few words are written in the biblical text about these horses ... A good reason to use our imaginations to fill in the details, or reason to be more careful in what we conclude about this quartet?

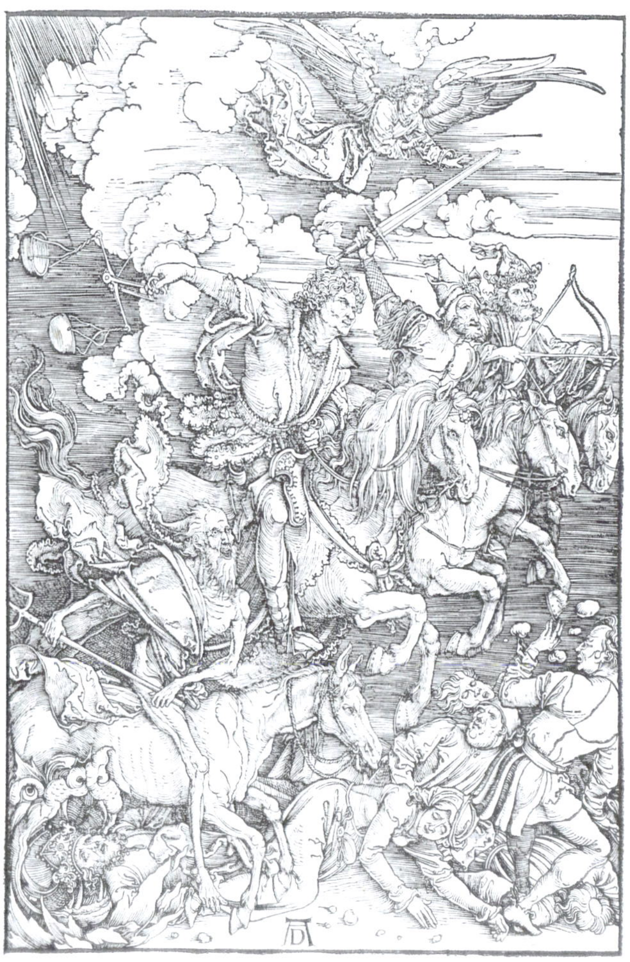

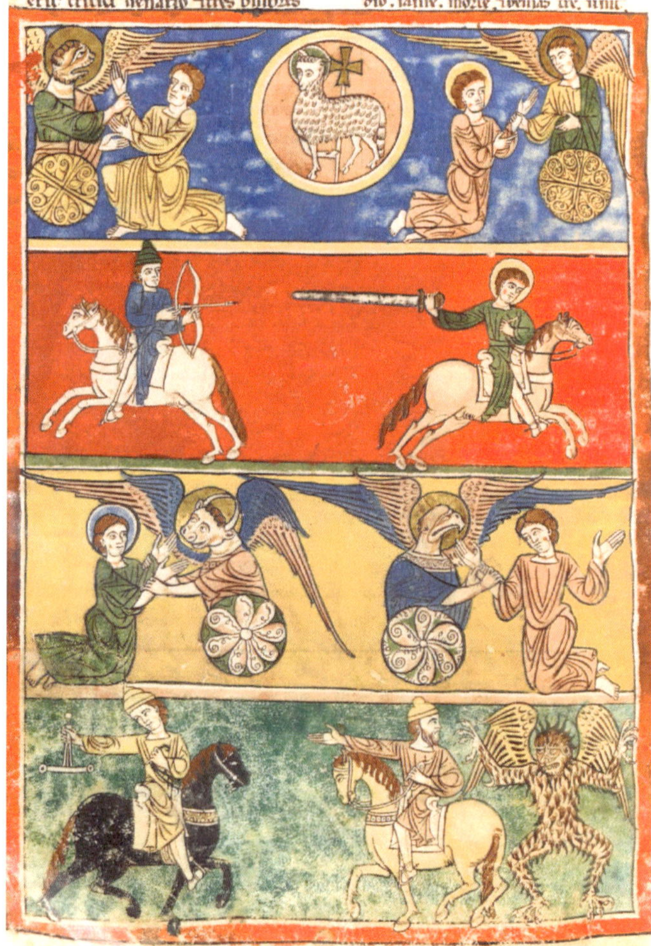

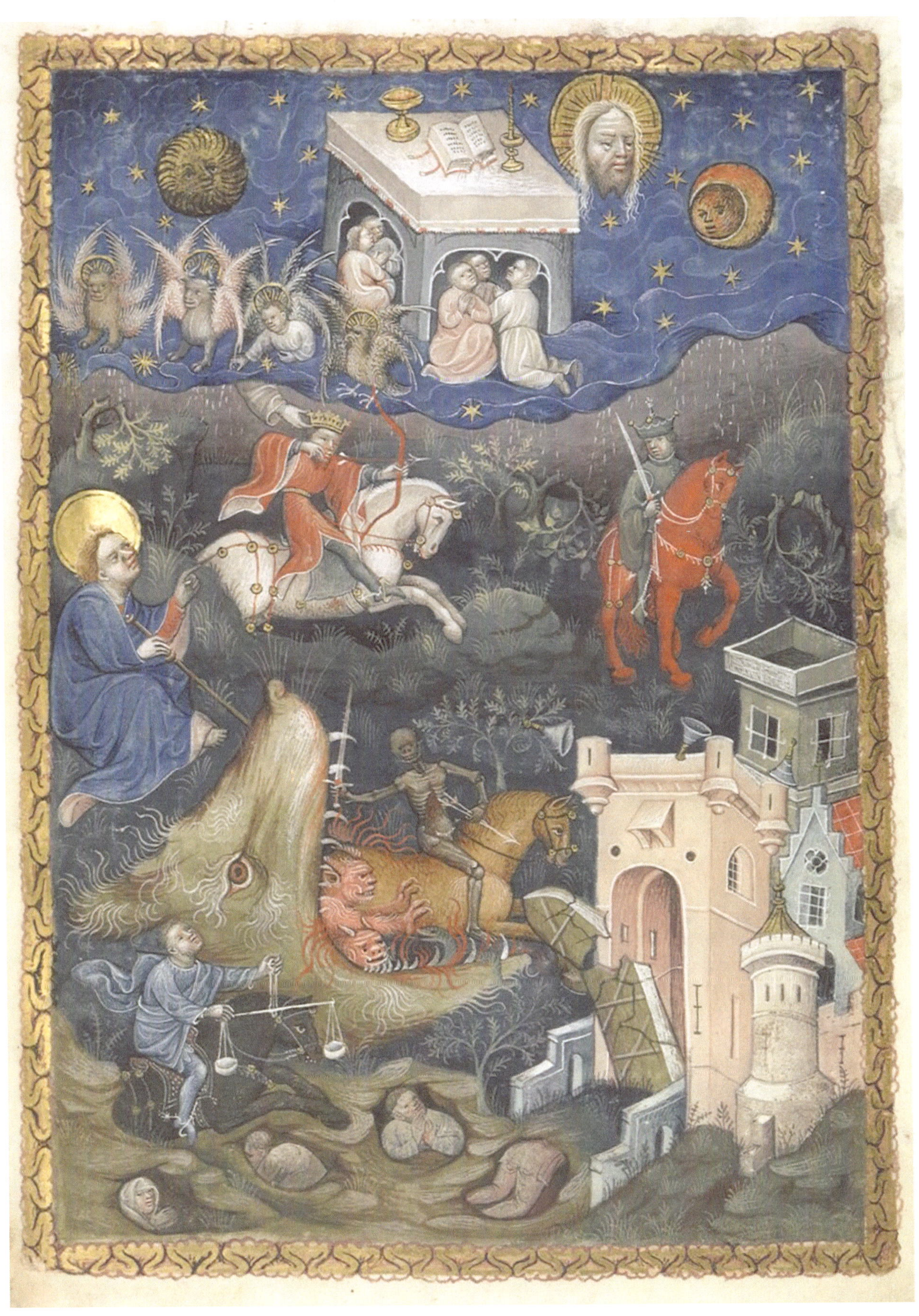

First Unsealing

> *6: 1 Then I saw the Lamb open one of the seven seals, and I heard one of the four living creatures call out, as with a voice of thunder, "Come!" 2 I looked, and there was a white horse! Its rider had a bow; a crown was given to him, and he came out conquering and to conquer.*

Why a white horse? The colour white has been mentioned several times before and seems to signify victory, justification, purity, holiness, God Himself, His creatures and members of the churches. White always has a positive connotation. The horse is white because it is a horse with no evil intent (contra Beal and Boxall). Or, the horse could represent the people of God, as it does in Zechariah.

The Greek word translated "rider", is the same word used for the "Seated one" on the throne (Rev 4). We could say this rider is "enthroned" on the horse. So, we expect Christ or one of his servants. Many have believed this after Irenaeus (including recently Farrer, Leithart, Eaton, Ellul, Lenski and others). But the rider could also refer to the good news, God's word, or the Holy Spirit.

The rider goes to war with a victory wreath and crown on his head! Every church was told to conquer: to Laodicea Christ added that they had to do it in the same way He had (3:21). This conquest is primarily a spiritual one. [This line of thought will be affirmed when we get to Rev 19.]

Is this a "bow" or a rainbow? It seems a bow, and one assumes arrows, even though they are not mentioned. God handled bow and arrows in the OT as well (Hab 3:8).

In the *Trinity* painting below, the rider is Christ, and the application is to the people before the flood. The living creature is "like a man", unlike the order I follow (4:7), "like a lion".

My own painting is more dynamic. Galloping out of the open seal, the "seated one" with his rainbow-coloured bow reminds us of the first covenant with Noah. The Lamb is present, and the lion, and there is lots of noise. I kept changing my mind when reading these chapters. First I followed Caird, and many with him, who sees this horse as part of the rest. But are they too influenced by what comes next and read the trumpets and the bowl judgements into these seals? [Caird used the last horse to interpret all the others.]

Instead I see here the Holy Spirit and the church taking the good news into the world after Christ's "lifting up", symbolized by the white horse.

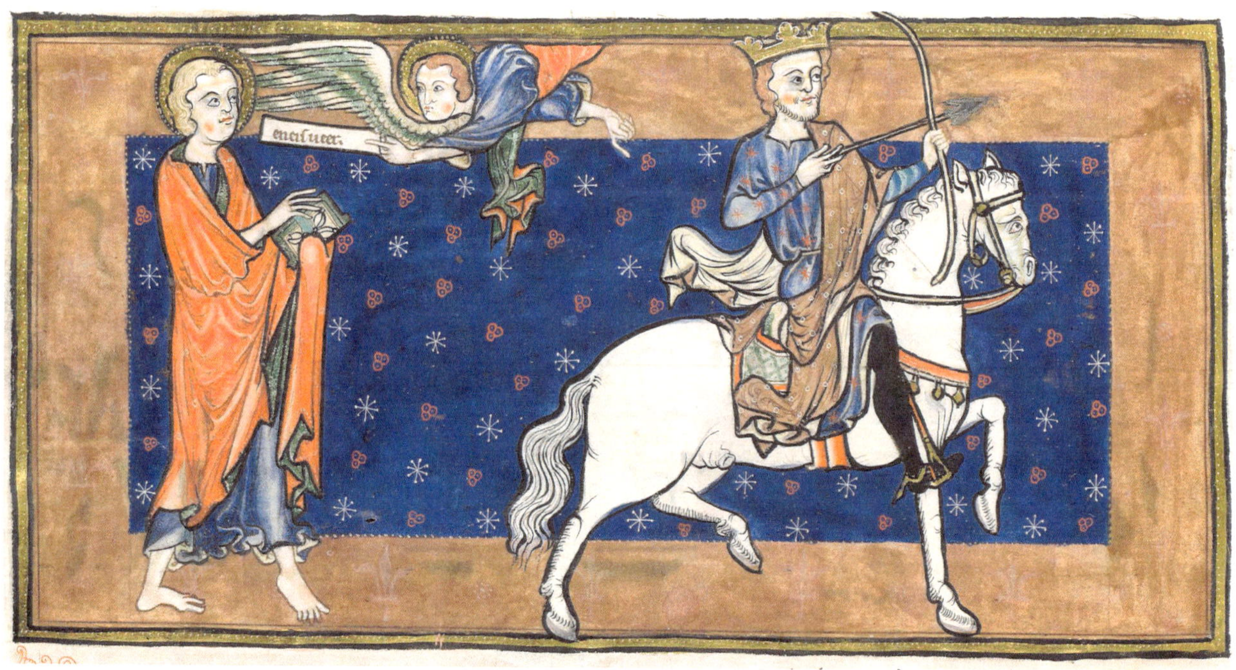

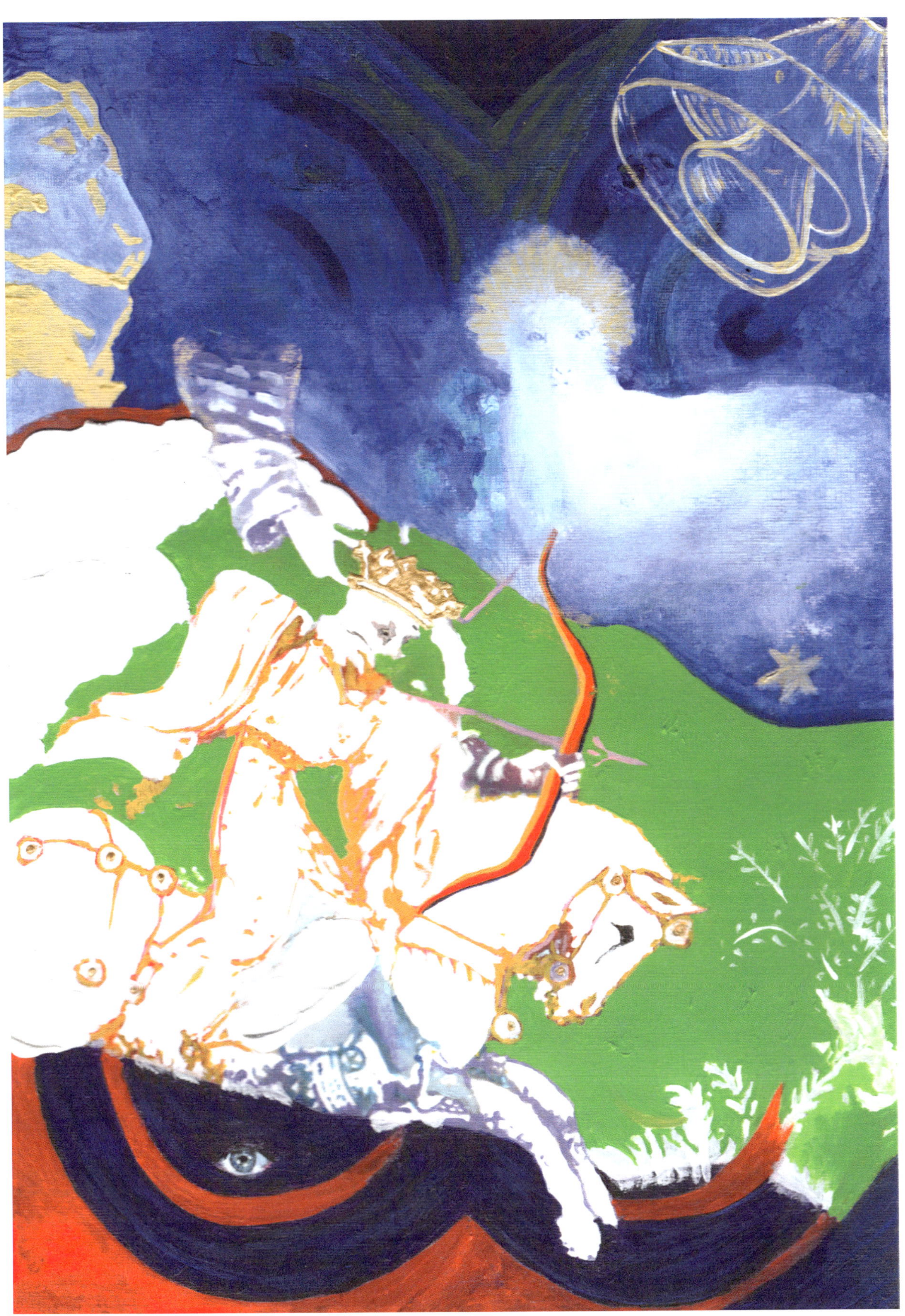

Second Unsealing

The noise levels are down. The second seal is opened. The second living creature calls out and a bright red horse appears.

This horse is permitted to take peace from the earth: people will slaughter one another. [This is the same "slaughter" the Lamb was subjected to, and the same "slaughter" that will link Him here and in the fifth unsealing to the martyrs.]

Why was the rider given a sword? To the church of Pergamum, Christ is said to have a sword coming out of his mouth. So we should consider the possibility the sword here is the word of God, even though a different "sword" is used here in the Greek. Aune says that the sword in Christ's mouth was a short sword or dagger, while here it is a long sword used for cutting and piercing. According to Koester the two words are used interchangeably in Revelation. Also note that the rider does not kill anyone: people kill one another.

Is this the continuing spiritual battle "not against flesh and blood" or does this refer to the division of families ("I have not come to bring peace", Jesus said) and the persecution of the saints? I think both are included here. But there is no great action yet. [It is as if we are introduced to the main players before the action explodes.]

Modern commentators find it hard to look beyond our daily newspaper reports of wars. Life in the first century also dripped with blood, for example Parthians against Romans. But, we remind ourselves, his is prophecy addressed to the churches.

6: [3]When he opened the second seal, I heard the second living creature call out, "Come!" [4]And out came another horse, bright red; its rider was permitted to take peace from the earth, so that people would slaughter one another; and he was given a great sword.

Why a bright red horse? Red is the colour of sacrifice, blood and warfare.

In my painting I introduce the blood of Christ-the-Lamb to link the slaughters and discord. All is set against the background of the seven horns, the symbol of Christ's utter strength.

The *Trinity* painting is similar to the previous one. The living creature this time is "like a lion", but in my painting like a bull.

Whatever is happening here is unleashed by Christ, to fulfil His purpose. He is in full control. The white horse has been released; the red horse shows there will be no peace as the gospel moves into the world. There will be strife and slaughter.

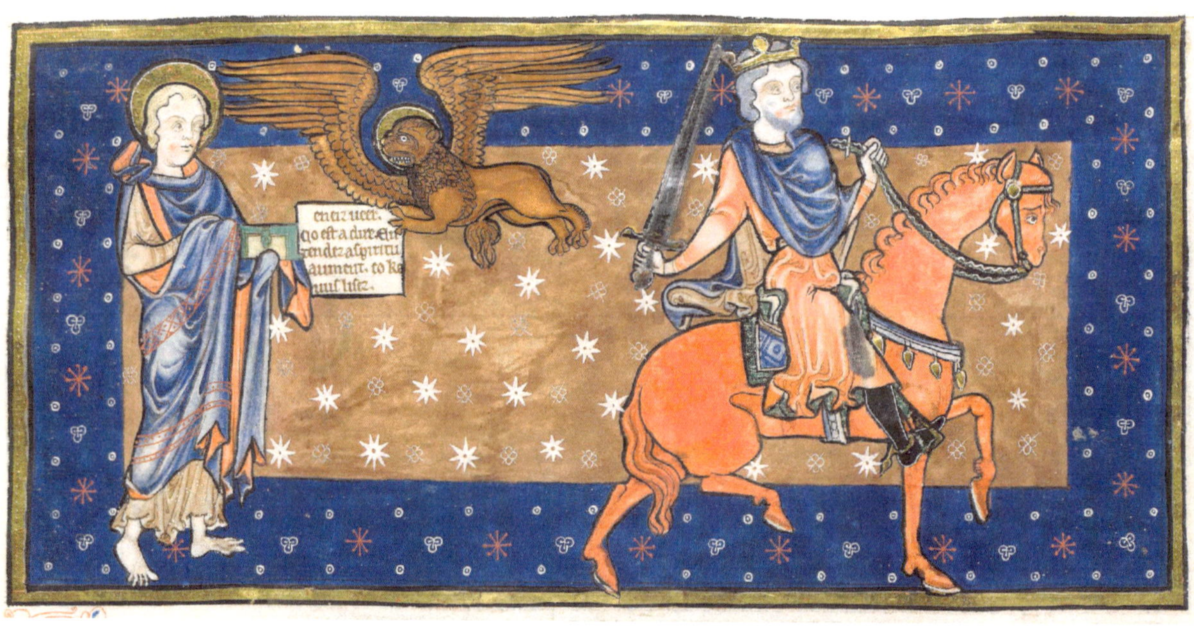

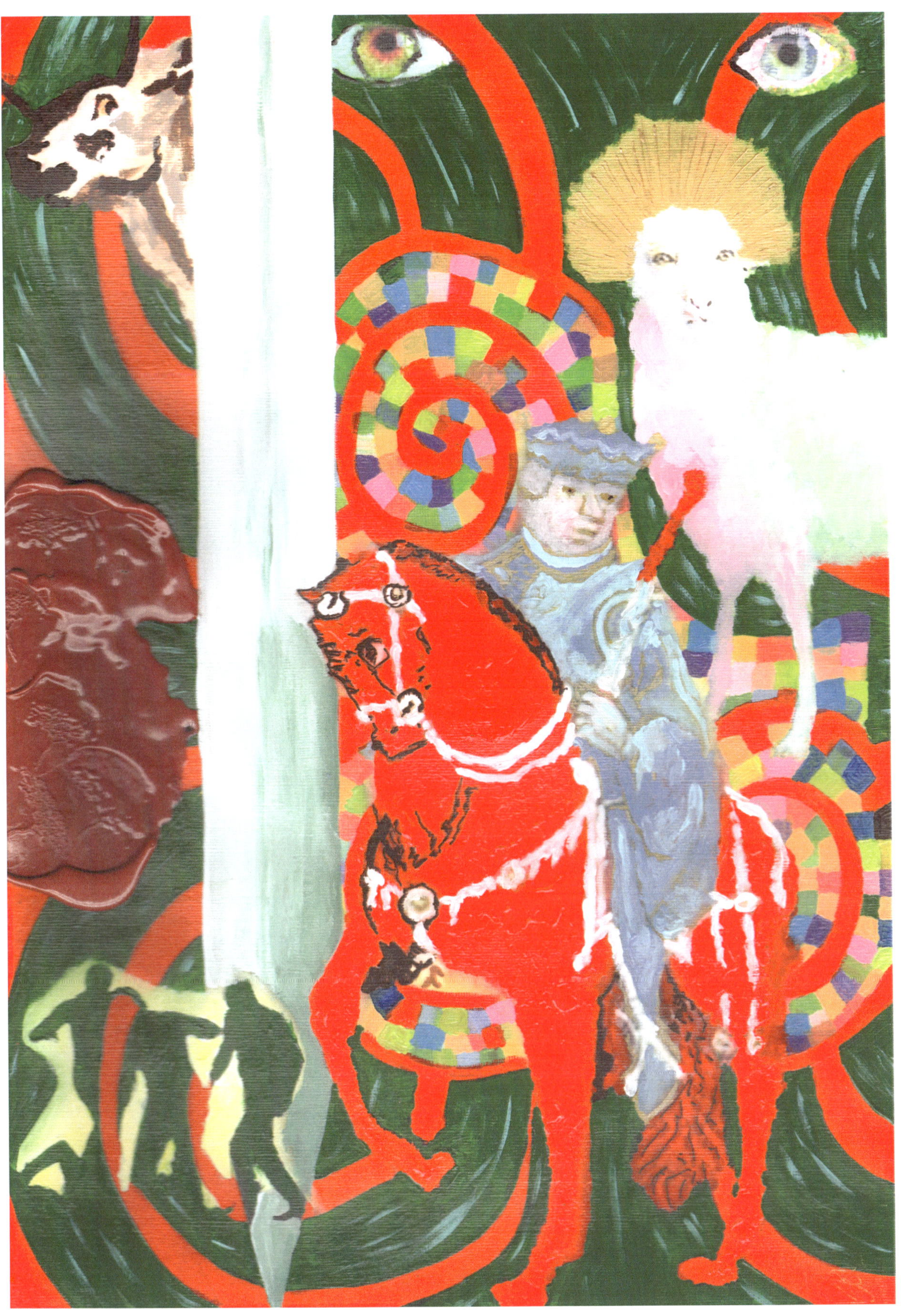

Third Unsealing

> *6: [5]When he opened the third seal, I heard the third liv-*
> *ing creature call out, "Come!" I looked, and there was a*
> *black horse! Its rider held a pair of scales in his hand,*
> *[6]and I heard what seemed to be a voice in the midst*
> *of the four living creatures saying, "A quart of wheat*
> *for a day's pay, and three quarts of barley for a day's*
> *pay, but do not damage the olive oil and the wine!"*

The Lamb opens the third seal, and a black horse appears at the command of the third creature ("like a man" in my painting). This rider holds a pair of scales. But to go into battle at speed carrying a pair of scales, as Dürer depicted it in his *Four Horsemen*, makes no sense.

Modern commentators see here mostly severe famine. As a result, food must be sold by weight, at prices no one can afford. But even in the first century scales also represented justice, and I think we need to read this more in line with the miscarriage of justice, as Lenski argues. The rich have enough to eat, but the poor though they work all day can hardly afford to buy food. It is not hard to see this black horse roaming across our world today (or any of the other horses).

The *Trinity* painting below has the black horse standing and the creature "like a bull" making the announcement addressed to "the Doctors of the [Mosaic] Law". Also notice that in the *Trinity* series every horse is enthroned by Christ.

In my painting I link the blood of Christ here with the scales and the seven eyes that see everything. I interpret the black horse as the horse of injustice, particularly on poor Christians who are disenfranchised by the world because of their testimony of Christ, then and now and, apparently, into the future. [This theme will be developed.] But the black horse and his "seated one" are not allowed to damage olive oil and wine, staples also in those days.

Why a black horse? There is not much clarity about the meaning of the colour black. It is hardly mentioned in the OT, and then only to describe hair. The black horses in Zechariah are on their way to the north, but there seems no particular significance attached to their colour. Stefanovic helpfully suggests that in Revelation, black is related to darkness: the sun becomes "black as sackcloth" (6:12). In the NT, darkness symbolizes the absence of the gospel (see Matt 4:16; John 1:5; 3:19).

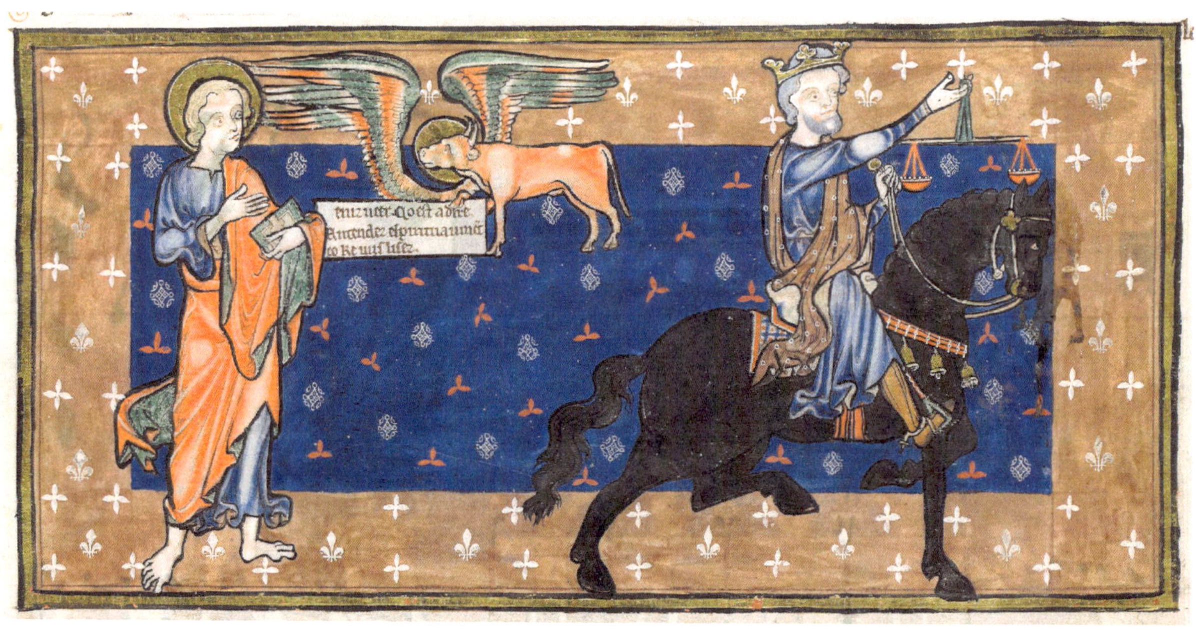

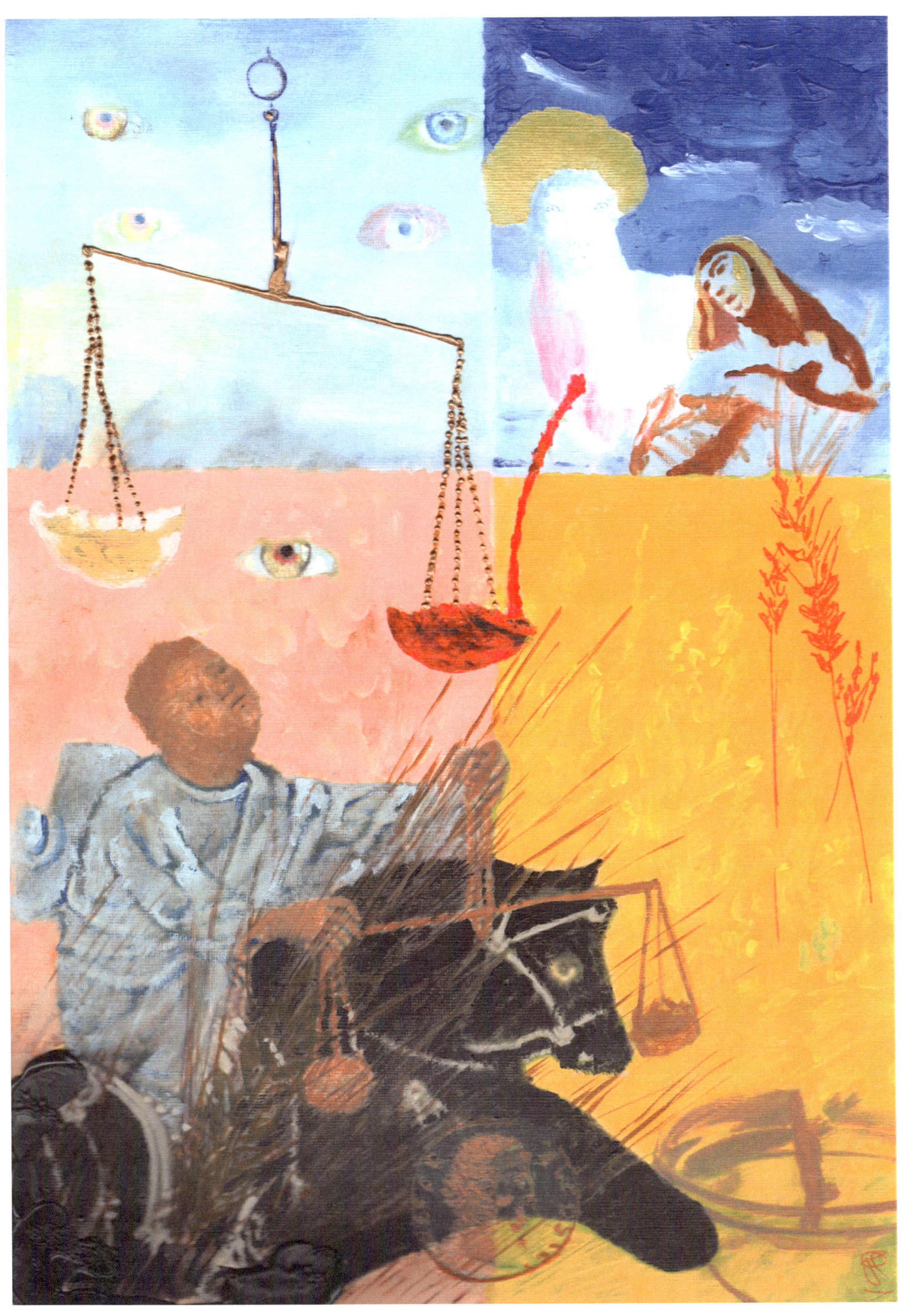

Fourth Unsealing

6: [7]When he opened the fourth seal, I heard the voice of the fourth living creature call out, "Come!" [8]I looked and there was a pale green horse! Its rider's name was Death, and Hades followed with him; they were given authority over a fourth of the earth, to kill with sword, famine, and pestilence, and by the wild animals of the earth.

The fourth creature, like a flying eagle (in both my painting and the *Trinity* one below), calls up the last horse: a pale green one. Its "seated one" is named "Death and Hades". We are left in no doubt what this refers to. But that has not stopped the painters of the *Trinity* to portray this rider, too, as Christ (Leithart also takes this view). Hades is portrayed below with demons and a big open mouth swallowing up lost people.

Why a pale-green horse? The word here, *chlōros*, refers to green grass in 8:7, but it was also used in ancient times to describe a person who was sick or dead.

In my own painting I copy the *Dietsche*, with death portrayed as the enemy it is shown to be in the Bible. In addition to the sword, famine (no growth), pestilence (the large viruses) and the wild beast (also Hades), I quoted the beheading by ISIS of Christians on a beach in Egypt. My understanding is that Christ, who is securely in charge of the keys of death and Hades, allows them to do their necessary work limited to a fourth of the earth.

The book of Revelation addresses the seven churches, so this is not a general prophecy but a message particularly for the church. Most commentators rightly refer to Ezekiel 14:21: "How much more when I send upon Jerusalem my four deadly acts of judgment, sword, famine, wild animals, and pestilence, to cut off humans and animals from it ...", which was also not a general announcement of judgement, but one very specific to the people of God in Jerusalem.

Eaton suggests that as the white horse (the preaching of the good news) goes out, the other horses show the consequences of preaching. Reading Eusebius's church history, I was struck by how the red, black and pale-green horses have been at work, as indeed they are today, wherever the gospel has gone out. Inevitably, slaughter, unjust persecution and death follow. Eusebius refers to Christian martyrs as "fulfilled" ones. I was moved by this. In *The China Chronicles*, Paul Hattaway shows how repeatedly throughout Chinese history, Christians have counted their lives "fulfilled" in this way.

The four horses do not bring the end of the world, at least not yet.

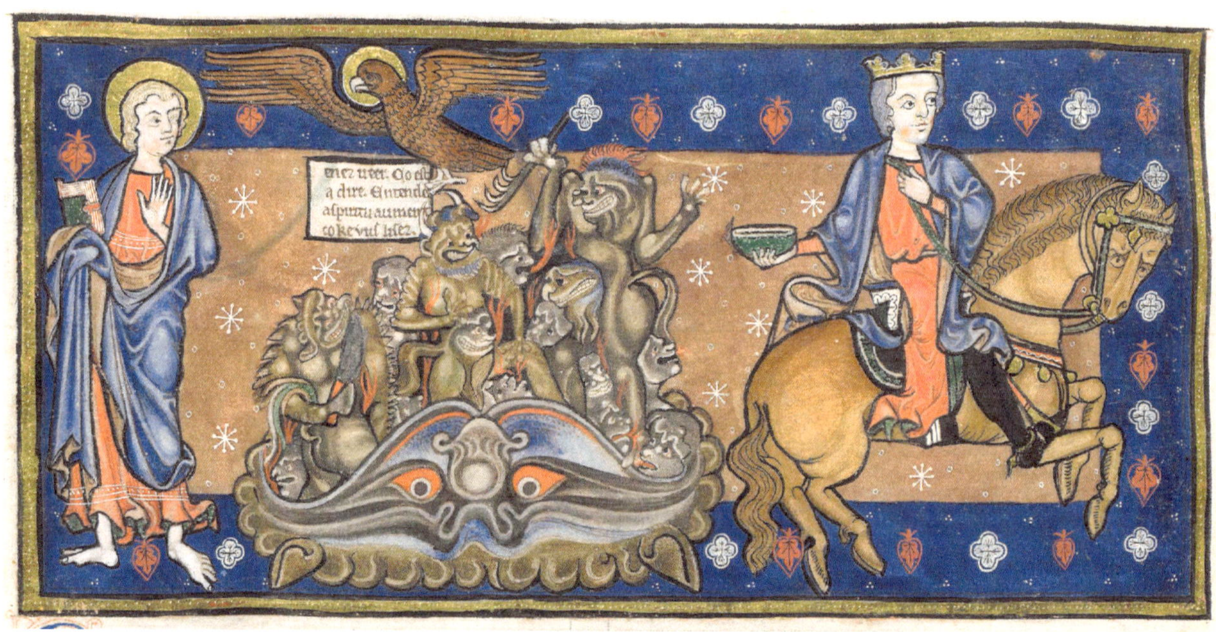

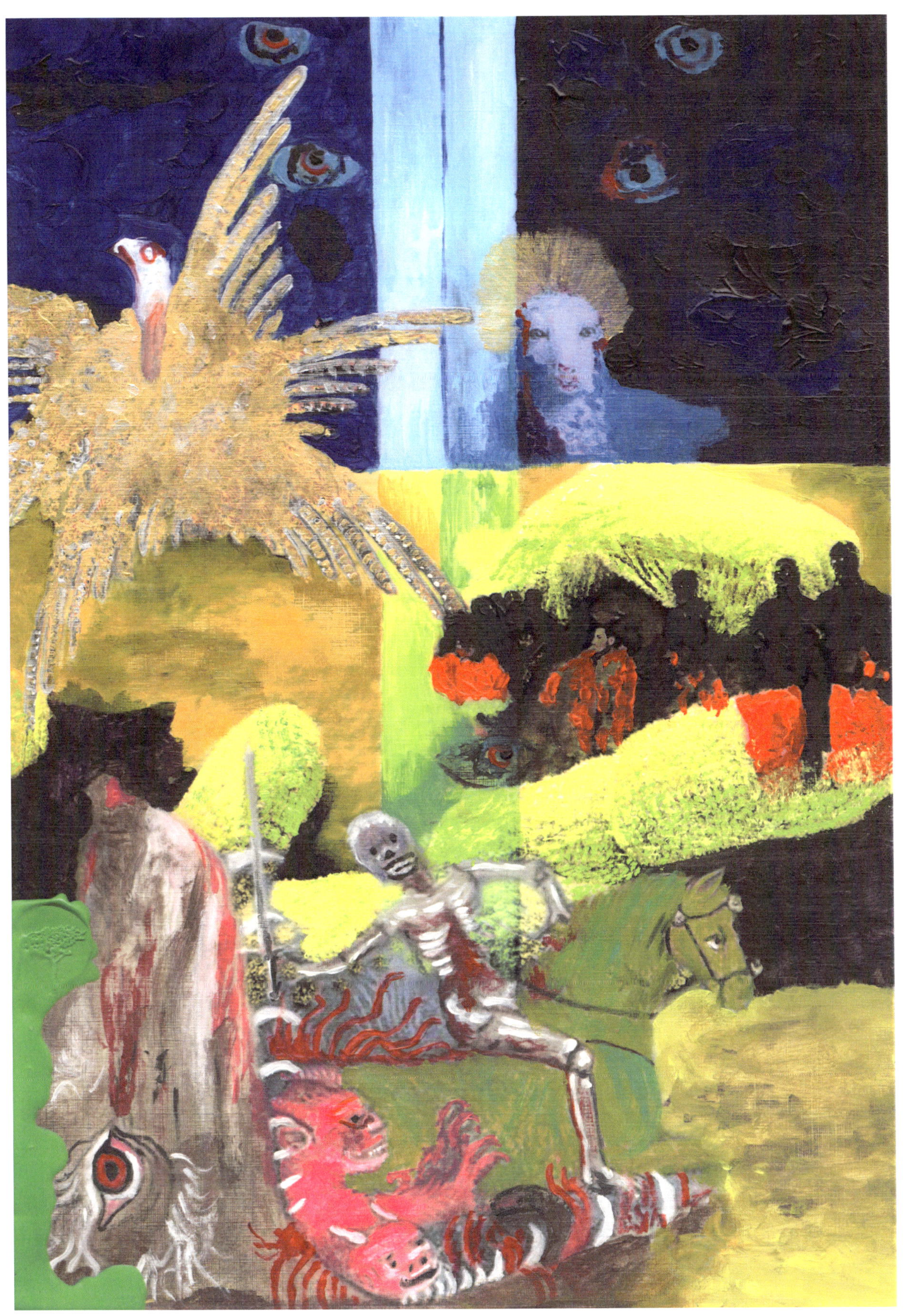

Fifth Unsealing

The opening of this seal follows very naturally on from the first four. It seems to me immaterial were John saw this "altar" in heaven or on earth. Many commentators wax eloquently about it, but John's emphasis seems to be on the martyrs and their cry.

> *6: [9]When he opened the fifth seal, I saw under the altar the souls of those who had been slaughtered for the word of God and for the testimony they had given; [10]they cried out with a loud voice, "Sovereign Lord, holy and true, how long will it be before you judge and avenge our blood on the inhabitants of the earth?" [11]They were each given a white robe and told to rest a little longer, until the number would be complete both of their fellow servants and of their brothers and sisters, who were soon to be killed as they themselves had been killed.*

"Slaughter" here refers to the slaughter of the Lamb and the slaughtering brought about by the red horse. I have visually shown this in my painting. The Lamb's blood is mixed with the blood of the martyrs. Some commentators suggest that John used the word "souls" for the blood. The slaughter is clearly connected to those who have conquered "as Christ has conquered", and they now cry "How long?" These martyrs, starting with Antipas (see 2:13), gave their lives as they witnessed to the word of God.

In my painting I portray their cry in the right-hand upper corner with a dim but hopeful sight of the new Jerusalem. Their white robes come from heaven, over the altar to cover them, probably a reference to their justification. The white seal is shown open in the bottom left corner.

Who are these martyrs? They appear to be a "first fruit" of early church martyrs. More will follow as we continue in Revelation, and on into our own time. There is yet no end in sight.

The *Getty* illustration below shows a very detailed clothing of the martyrs in white by the angels from heaven, and "souls" under the altar.

Vengeance belongs to the Lord, who alone is holy and true. The prayer of the martyrs is not a sign of personal vindictiveness but a cry for justice, a cry for God to finally put all wrongs to right. The perpetrators they implore God to avenge are the inhabitants of the earth [who we will come across again]. The martyrs are told to rest until their number is complete.

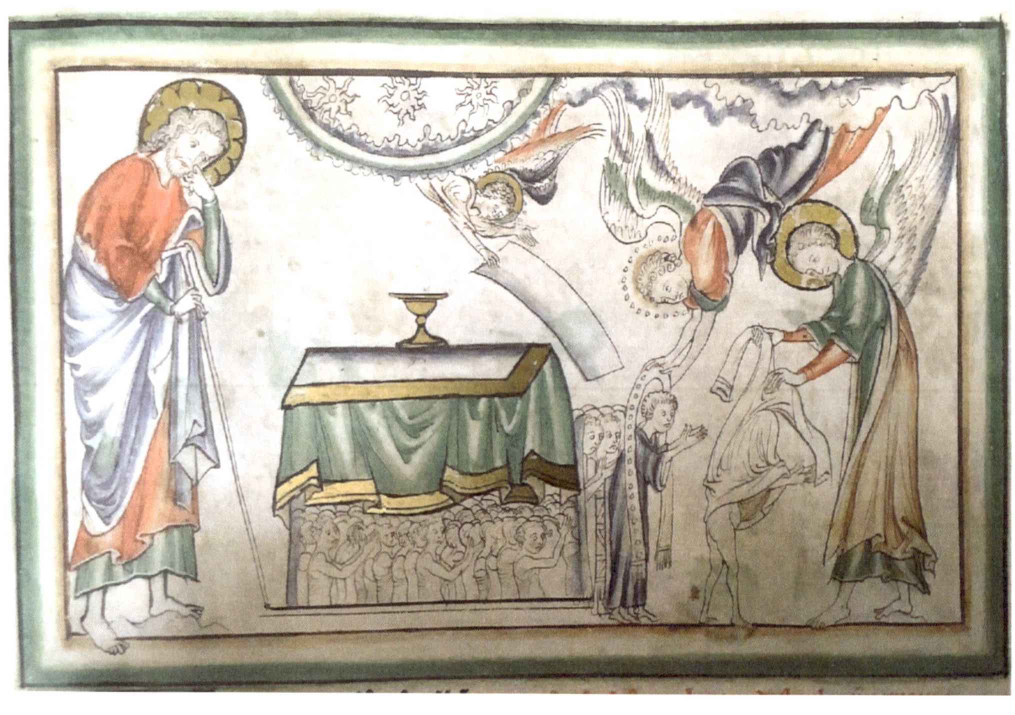

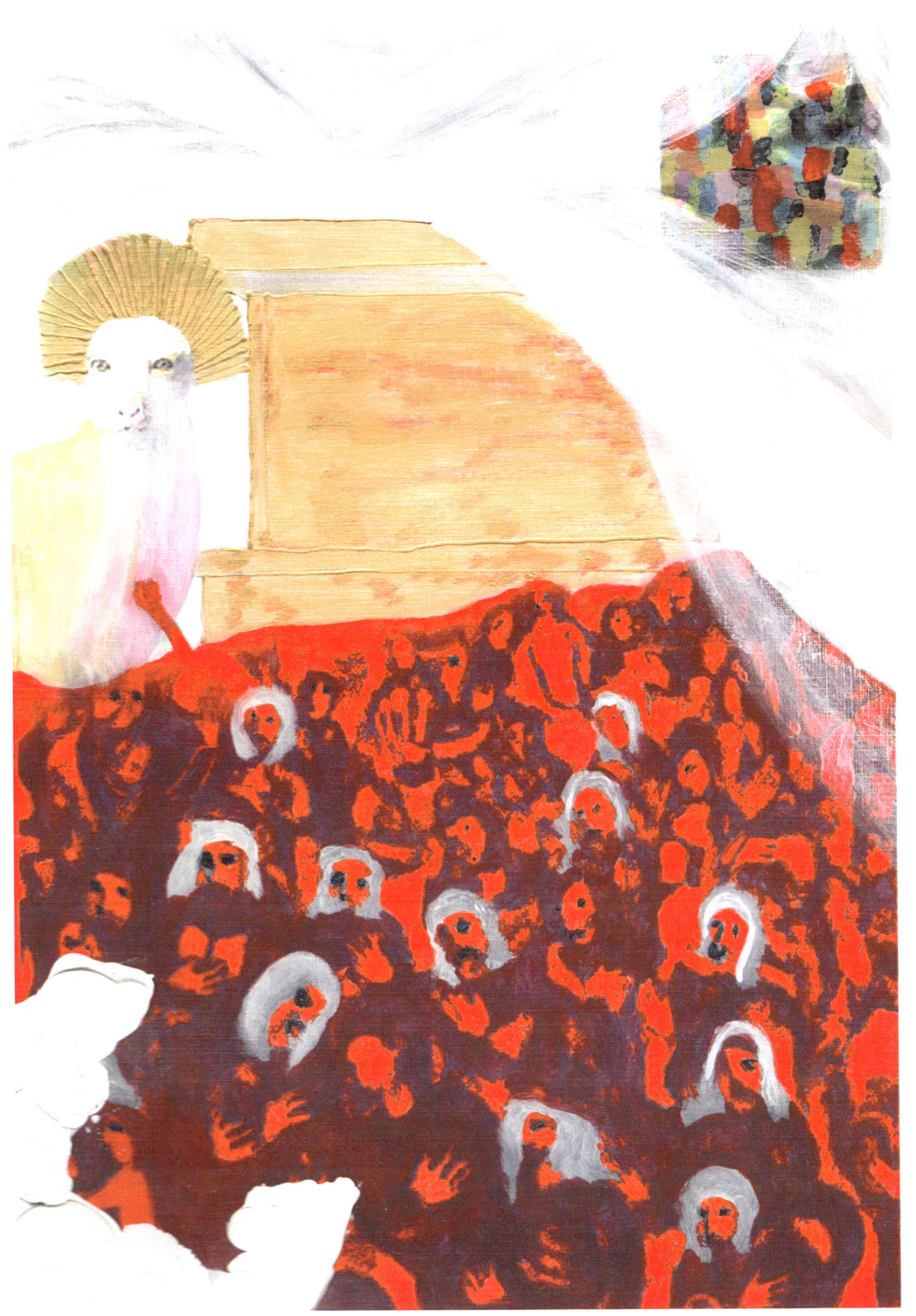

Sixth Unsealing

The sixth unsealing follows the fifth and focuses on what will happen to the inhabitants of the earth, over whom vengeance has been cried out at the opening of the fifth seal. It then adds three visions regarding the people of God and their salvation to portray the vindication of the church.

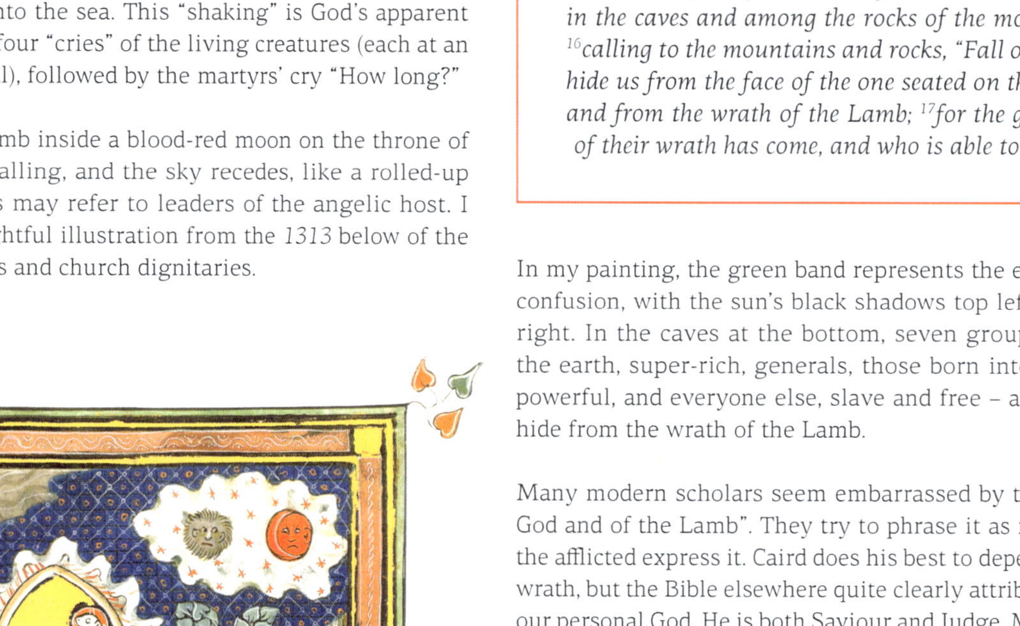

6: 12 When he opened the sixth seal, I looked, and there
came a great earthquake; the sun became black as
sackcloth, the full moon became like blood, 13 and the
stars of the sky fell to the earth as the fig tree drops its
winter fruit when shaken by a gale. 14 The sky vanished
like a scroll rolling itself up, and every mountain and
island was removed from its place. 15 Then the kings of
the earth and the magnates and the generals and the
rich and the powerful, and everyone, slave and free, hid
in the caves and among the rocks of the mountains,
16 calling to the mountains and rocks, "Fall on us and
hide us from the face of the one seated on the throne
and from the wrath of the Lamb; 17 for the great day
of their wrath has come, and who is able to stand?"

Lenski argues that we should not read "earthquake" here but just "quake" or "shake". The Lamb's opening of the scroll affects all of creation: in reverse motion, the sky is rolled up like a scroll! Not just islands, but mountains too are "undone" and disappear into the sea. This "shaking" is God's apparent response to the four "cries" of the living creatures (each at an opening of a seal), followed by the martyrs' cry "How long?"

I painted the Lamb inside a blood-red moon on the throne of God. Stars are falling, and the sky recedes, like a rolled-up scroll. The stars may refer to leaders of the angelic host. I quoted the insightful illustration from the *1313* below of the "hiding" of kings and church dignitaries.

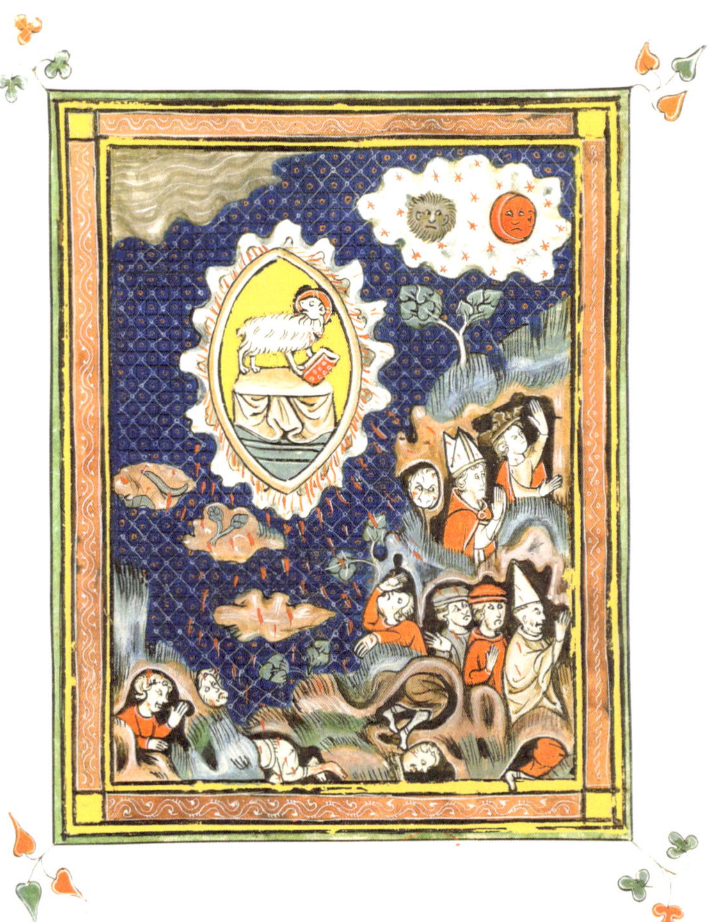

In my painting, the green band represents the earth in all its confusion, with the sun's black shadows top left and bottom right. In the caves at the bottom, seven groups – kings of the earth, super-rich, generals, those born into wealth, the powerful, and everyone else, slave and free – are rushing to hide from the wrath of the Lamb.

Many modern scholars seem embarrassed by this "wrath of God and of the Lamb". They try to phrase it as merely a way the afflicted express it. Caird does his best to depersonalize the wrath, but the Bible elsewhere quite clearly attributes wrath to our personal God. He is both Saviour and Judge. Many scholars see this opening as a description of the future final judgement day and its appearance here as a proleptic instance. It is firmly connected to Matthew 24, Mark 13 and Luke 21 which can either refer to the fall of Jerusalem or the Parousia. Many take it to be the latter.

This event cannot be a "literal" happening, but this kind of language is used in the Bible to signify major change and often in the OT, major political change. So this describes the coming ending of "a world", though not necessarily the final end of "the world" and echoes Isaiah 2:11–19 and Joel 2.

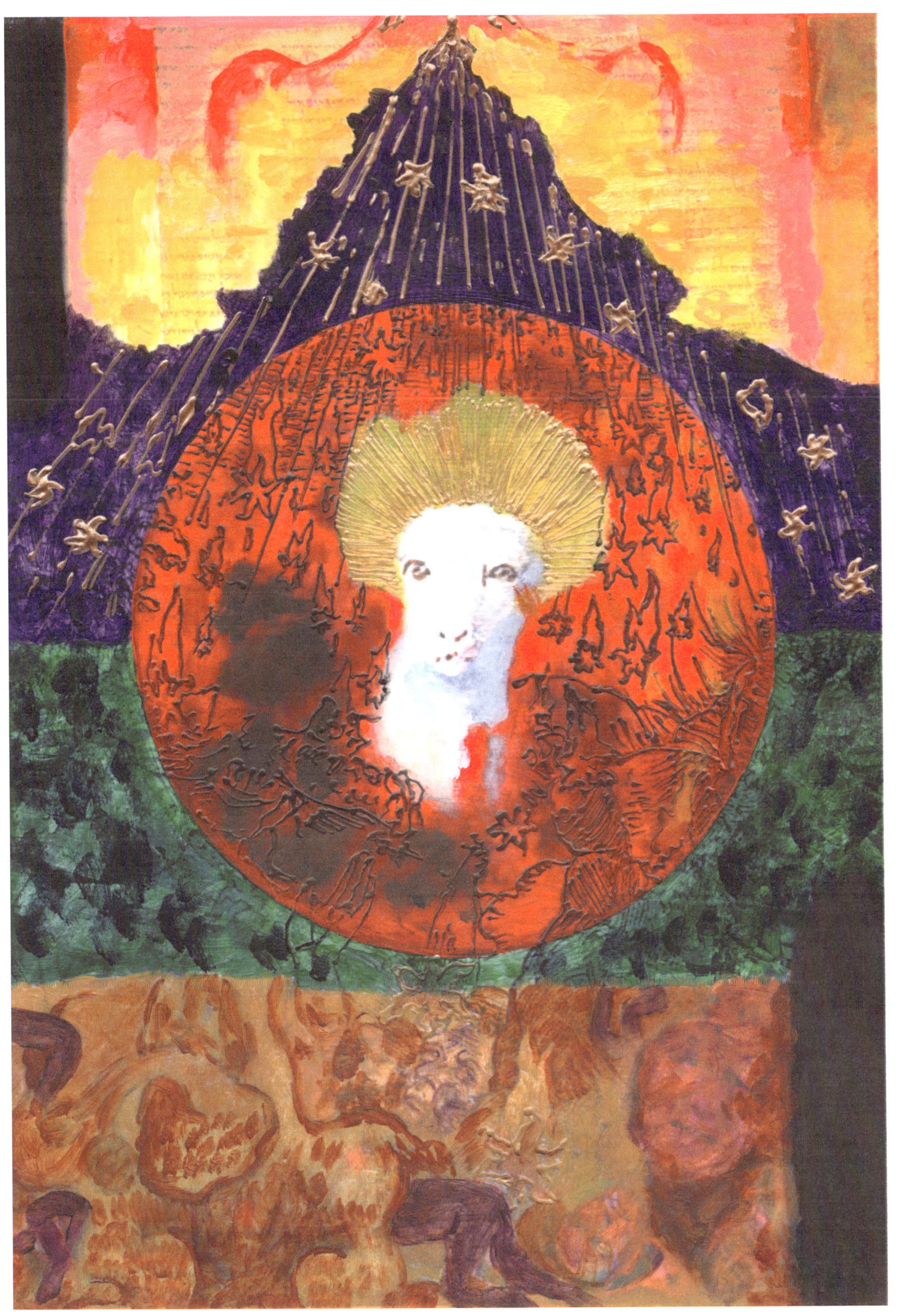

Sealing Servants

> *7: 1After this I saw four angels standing at the four*
> *corners of the earth, holding back the four winds of*
> *the earth so that no wind could blow on earth or sea*
> *or against any tree. 2I saw another angel ascending*
> *from the rising of the sun, having the seal of the living*
> *God, and he called with a loud voice to the four angels*
> *who had been given power to damage earth and sea,*
> *3saying, "Do not damage the earth or the sea or the*
> *trees, until we have marked the servants of our God*
> *with a seal on their foreheads."*

The opening of the sixth seal is not finished yet. Two additional visions address "Who will be able to stand?"

I love the *Getty* illustration below, with the angels holding the "winds" and covering the winds' mouths with their hands. The "angel" on the right we are told is Christ, holding a document addressed to the angels and sealed with the sign of the sun. Its command not to damage earth and sea and tree reminds us of the restrictions placed on the black horse.

Who are the angels? We have limited information, but they are clearly angels and not evil demons! "Another" angel is just another angel, not "another kind". God can use his angels for good and ill, and He may allow demonic forces to operate as well [more about this later].

Many commentators connect the four winds with the four horsemen, based on Zechariah 1 and 6. I think this fails to honour that John is writing what he saw! God uses the visual vocabulary of the OT as rich echoes. His answer to the question includes that not a breeze will disrupt the angels' sealing of His people!

What is this seal marking God's servants? We are not told, but it comes from the living God. It reminds me of the Holy Spirit's seal of ownership and authentication: "In him you also, when you had heard the word of truth, the gospel of your salvation, and had believed in him, were marked with the seal of the promised Holy Spirit; this is the pledge of our inheritance toward redemption as God's own people, to the praise of his glory" (Eph 1:13–14). Later in Revelation it will be linked with the name of God, which I anticipate in my painting on the forehead of John (whom I imagine as the first sealed). I also considered the cross, instead of the "tree of life" on the seals.

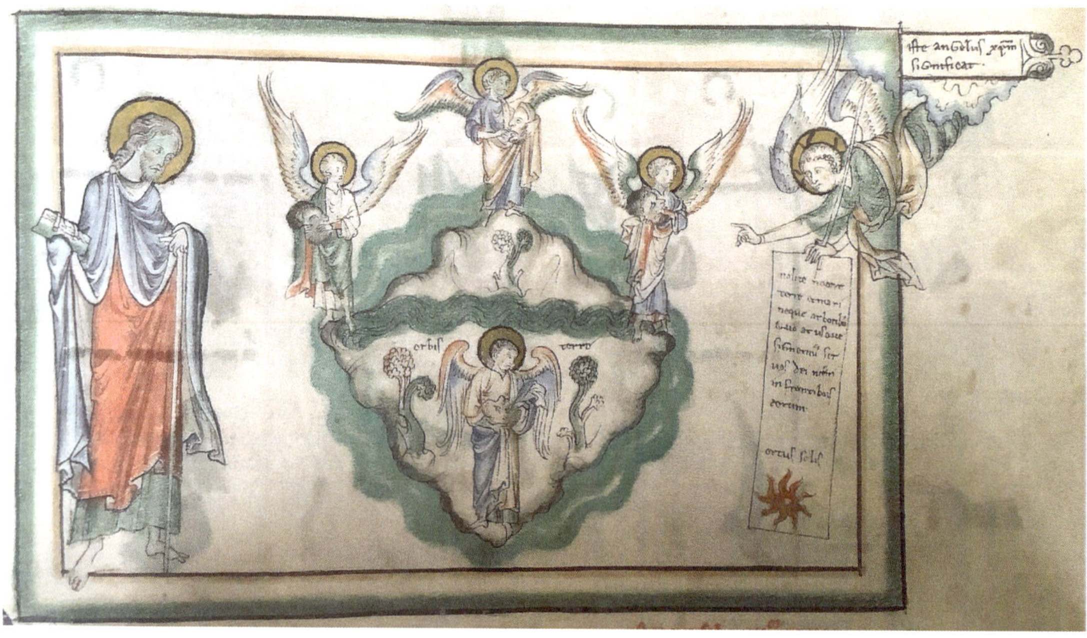

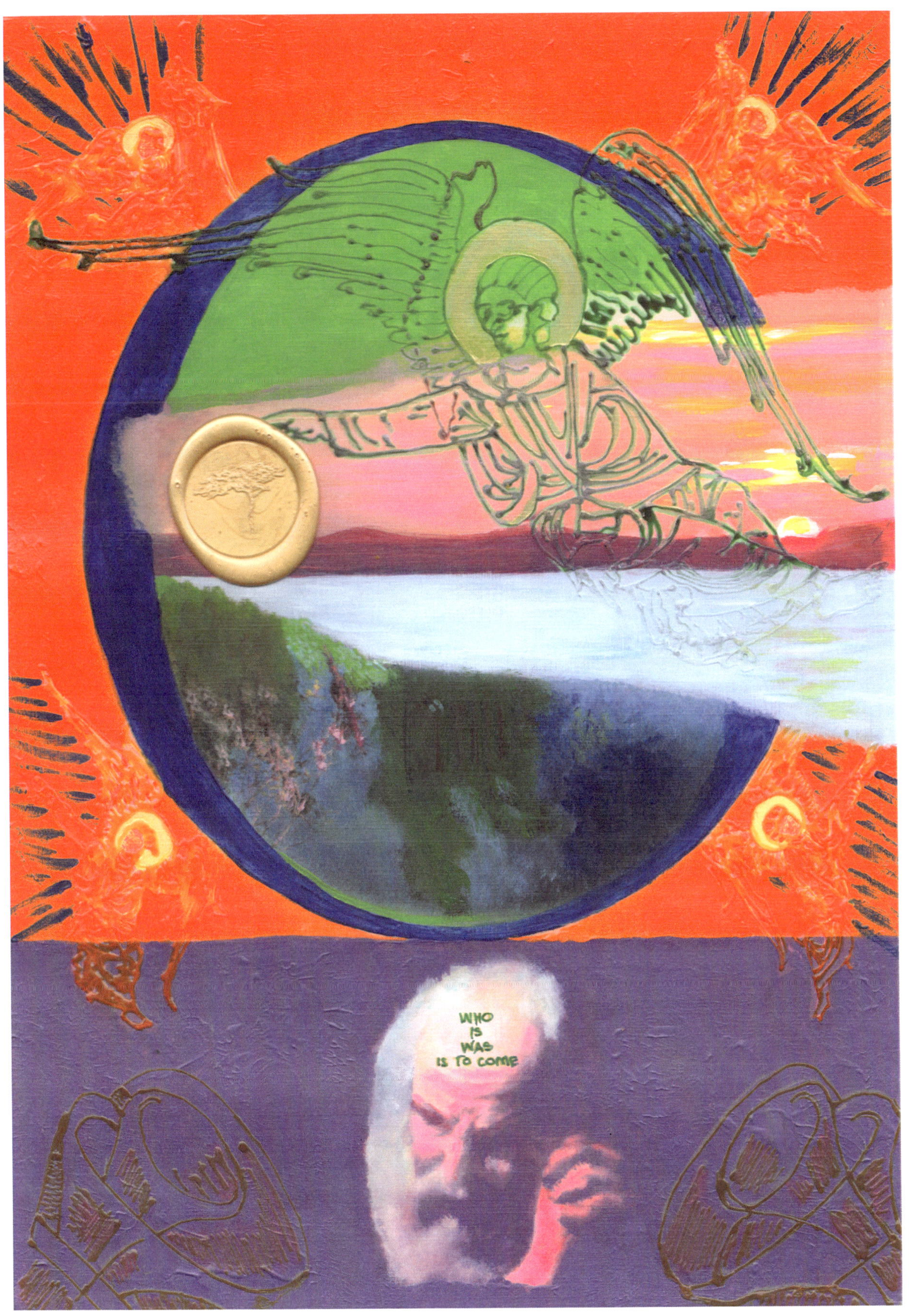
WHO
IS
WAS
IS TO COME

144,000

John did not see this as a "vision" but heard it! When I read this text I tried to visualize it and immediately thought of Mondrian and Vasarely. I asked Nazar Soloviy, our lodger and expert in all things mathematical, how to combine a 12 x 12 square and a 10 x 10 x 10 cube. It was an unsolvable enigma. In the end we settled on a square grid of 120 x 120, forming one tenth of the whole, so to appreciate the number 144,000 you will have to put 10 of my paintings next to each other. I built the grid with paint and proceeded to put 14,400 drops of paint in the tiny squares.

I see this vision of the 144,000 as looking back to how the Israelites in Numbers surrounded the tabernacle: so in my painting there are twelve rectangles depicting the tribes. But the text also looks forward to the new Jerusalem: so I inserted a "holy" square (which should have been a cube) containing a full, circular rainbow with a golden centre representing the presence of God.

The stamp at the bottom is a real wax stamp, authenticating the work.

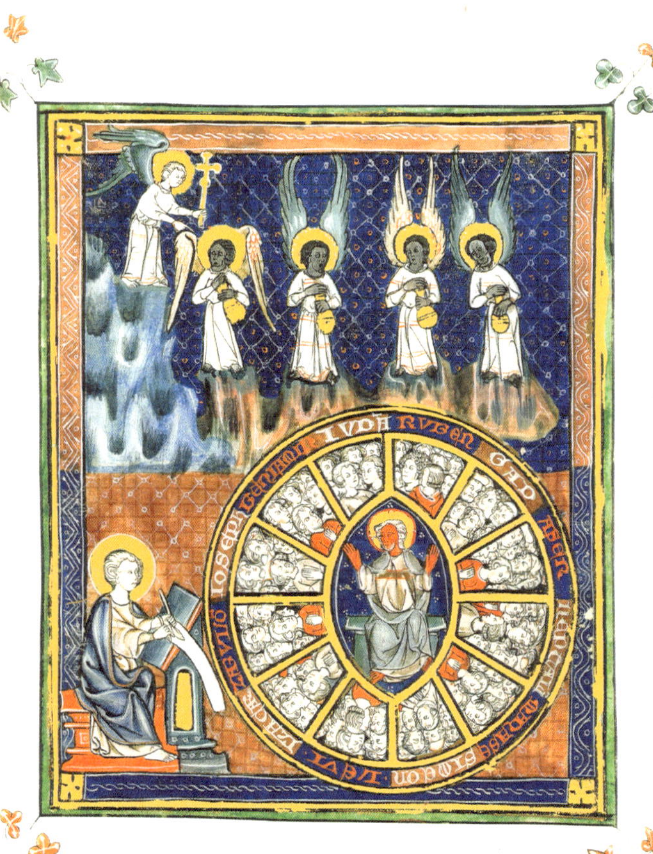

7: [4]And I heard the number of those who were sealed,
one hundred forty-four thousand, sealed out of every
tribe of the people of Israel:
[5]from the tribe of Judah twelve thousand sealed,
from the tribe of Reuben twelve thousand,
from the tribe of Gad twelve thousand,
[6]from the tribe of Asher twelve thousand,
from the tribe of Naphtali twelve thousand,
from the tribe of Manasseh twelve thousand,
[7]from the tribe of Simeon twelve thousand,
from the tribe of Levi twelve thousand,
from the tribe of Issachar twelve thousand,
[8]from the tribe of Zebulun twelve thousand,
from the tribe of Joseph twelve thousand,
from the tribe of Benjamin twelve thousand sealed.

The *1313* Illustration below is very fetching. It combines the opening verses, the four angels and the twelve tribes in a circular golden frame around the mandorla. This too looks forward to the new Jerusalem, where the gates are named after the tribes.

There is much debate about the list of tribes. It seems to me a Christianized version of the list. (Maybe implying that those grafted in are now part of the tribes.) Farrer and Bauckham are most eloquent about this.

Who are these twelve tribes? Are they Christian Jews? Are they Jewish Christian martyrs? Are they exactly the same group as the great multitude that will be mentioned next? It seems to me that the last suggestion makes the most sense.

Why 144,000? The 144,000 is a symbolic way of describing the whole people of God, including all those who have been "grafted in". It looks backwards and forwards as it symbolically refers to the twelve apostles [to be revealed as the foundations of the new Jerusalem] and the twelve tribes [to be revealed as the pearly gates of the new Jerusalem] and a 10 x 10 x 10 cube [symbolically representing both the holy of holies and the new Jerusalem].

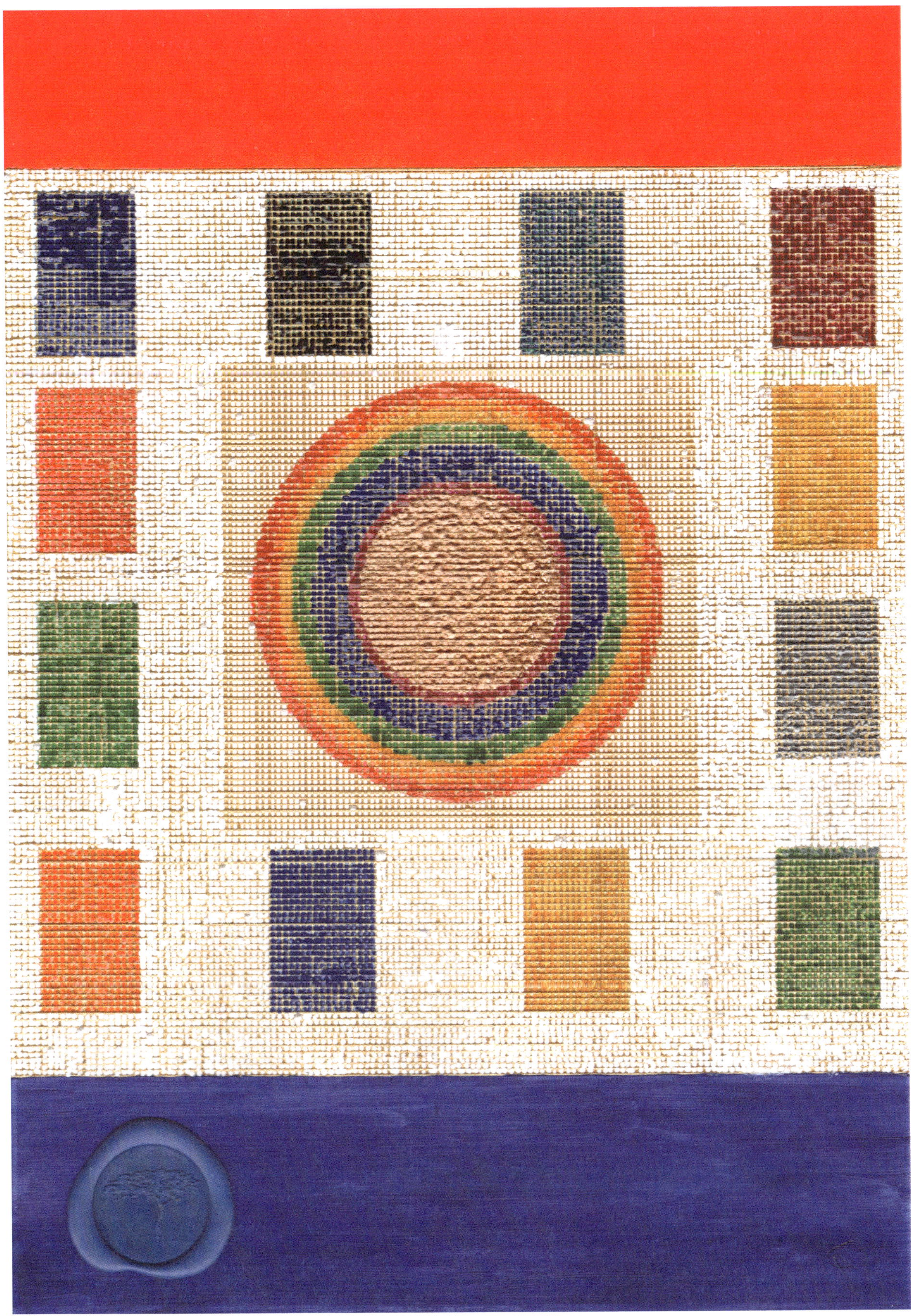

A Great Multitude

A third vision follows the sixth seal. It gives the answer to Who will be able to stand? Those who have come through the great ordeal.

This is the third time we encounter worship in heaven. In Revelation 4 it surrounded the throne and focused on the "Seated one". In Revelation 6 it focused on the Lamb and His redemption. This time it emphasizes the throne and the Lamb, but is focused on the worshippers: from every nation, tribe, people and language waving their palm branches.

In my painting I have tried to create the idea of a crowd, quoting Chagall and a photo I took in Nagaland. Further I reused the angels drawn by my grand-daughter Zhara, as well as images from my other paintings. The effect of the green palm branches on a yellow background has made this a very happy painting.

Kaai's painting is more sombre. I love the way she has depicted the crowd, and blue seems to be a good choice. I also like her very effective reflection shimmering from the throne.

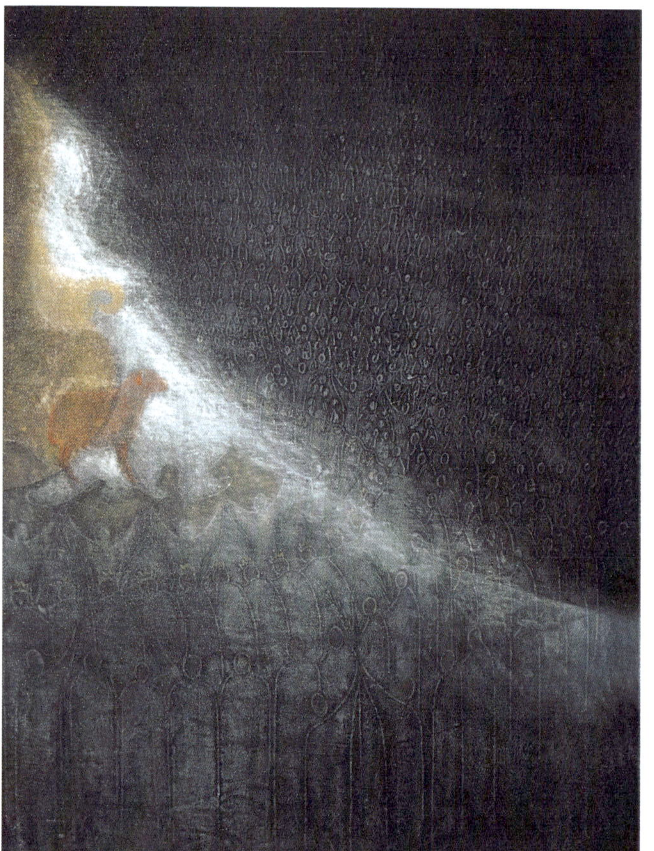

7: [9]After this I looked, and there was a great multitude
that no one could count, from every nation, from all
tribes and peoples and languages, standing before the
throne and before the Lamb, robed in white, with palm
branches in their hands. [10]They cried out in a loud
voice, saying, "Salvation belongs to our God who is
seated on the throne, and to the Lamb!"
[11]And all the angels stood around the throne and
around the elders and the four living creatures, and
they fell on their faces before the throne and worshiped
God, [12]singing,
"Amen! Blessing and glory and wisdom and thanks-
giving and honor
and power and might be to our God forever and
ever! Amen."
[13]Then one of the elders addressed me, saying, "Who
are these, robed in white, and where have they come
from?" [14]I said to him, "Sir, you are the one that
knows." Then he said to me, "These are they who have
come out of the great ordeal; they have washed their
robes and made them white in the blood of the Lamb.
[15]For this reason they are before the throne of God,
and worship him day and night within his temple,
and the one who is seated on the throne will shelter
them.
[16]They will hunger no more, and thirst no more;
the sun will not strike them, nor any scorching heat;
[17]for the Lamb at the center of the throne will be
their shepherd,
and he will guide them to springs of the water of life,
and God will wipe away every tear from their eyes."

Who is this great multitude? If they are, as I think, the same as the 144,000, they are the sealed ones who have come through the great ordeal. If not, we have to imagine them sealed, as we are not told they are!

What is the great ordeal? This is a tricky question. Many interpret this as the last and biggest ordeal before the Parousia of Christ. Others, and I include myself, see this as the accumulation of ordeals across time, from the ascension of Christ (Rev 5) to the Parousia.

This vision shows the people of God in their present (then and now) heavenly glory. Clearly the end has not yet come, for there is another seal to be opened!

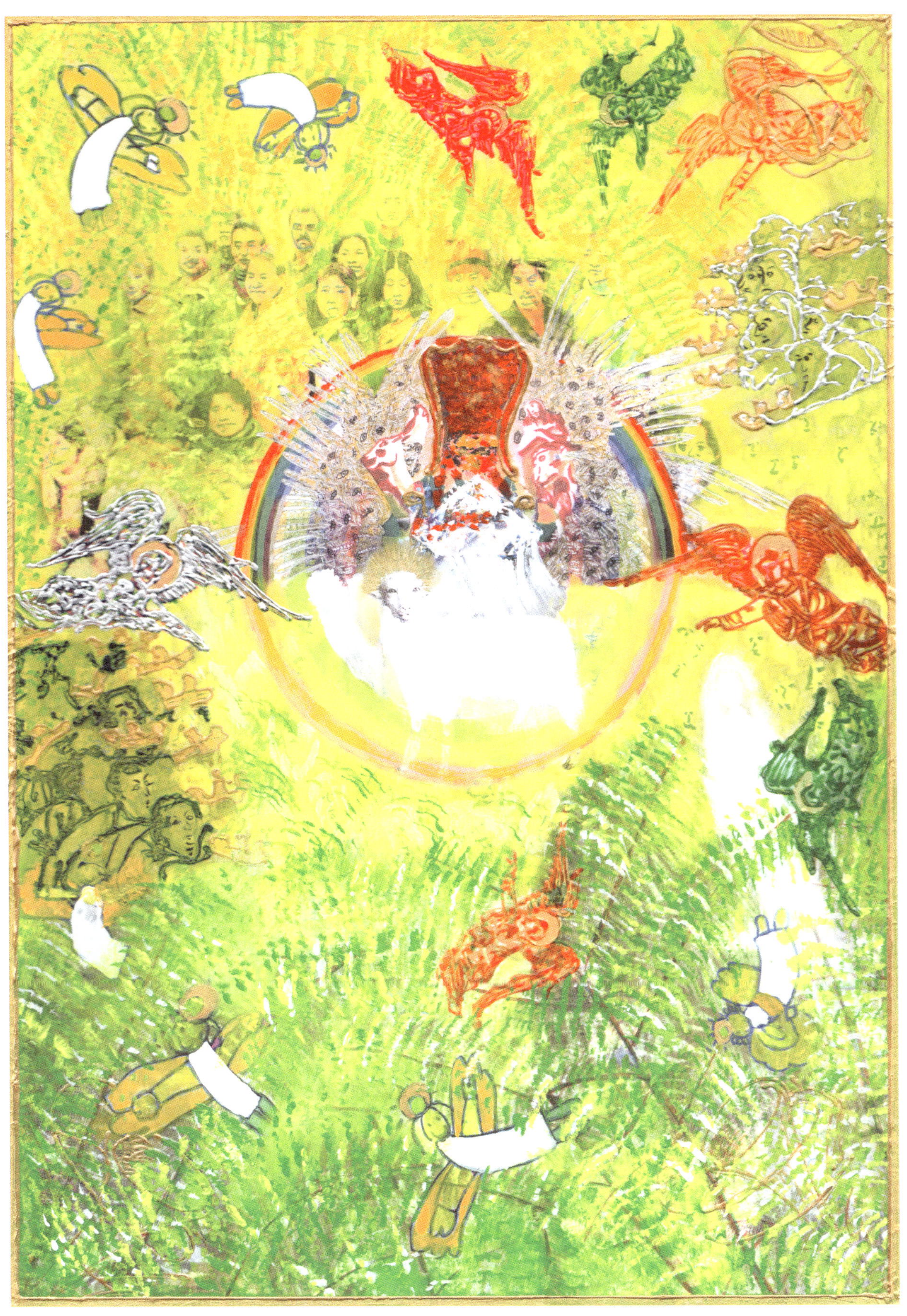

Seventh Unsealing

The opening of the seventh seal is somewhat of an anti-climax! Many commentators see it as just this one verse. The narrative however seems to continue, flowing into another liturgy. It seems to me that the opening of the seventh seal also contains the sounding of all the trumpets, which will initiate the action in all earnest.

But, before the action starts, there is a silence in heaven (not on earth). We have seen how noisy the worshippers and angels in heaven are just about all the time. But now, for half an hour, there is silence. This is what John hears; what he sees is seven angels quietly preparing around the altar.

I have painted a "half-time", a limited and shortened time. The blue evokes quietness, in contrast to brightly coloured activity. The angels are not at rest. They are quietly getting ready while they wait for the signal to get their trumpets and start making a noise again.

The *Getty* takes a similar approach, but its description is very different to how I read this. For the artists of the *Getty*, the giving of the trumpets relates to the birth of Christ. To them the silence is the peace under Octavius Augustus, under whose reign Christ was born. They interpret silence as peace. But silence is not peace nor sabbath. It is silence, time passing without any audible sound.

8: [1]When the Lamb opened the seventh seal, there was silence in heaven for about half an hour.

I think this quietness is at the very least an indication of anticipation. Heaven is waiting for God to say or do something. In my book it serves as a cliff-hanger, midway through the opening of the seventh seal. The action will DV start again in *Rainbow* 3 with Story Thirty-Three!

The half hour prepares us for the hour of judgement [to come, as in 14:7: "Fear God and give him glory, for the hour of his judgment has come."]. The half hour possibly suggests we are not quite there yet.

Some commentators suggest we use this "quiet" for prayer and worship as we wait for what comes next. Maybe you want to use it to write and/or draw your own meditation. I have painted and written a meditation in this frame of mind to consider what it means that the scroll has now been opened. I have also compiled a summary for myself of what I have learnt so far from the unsealing of all seven seals.

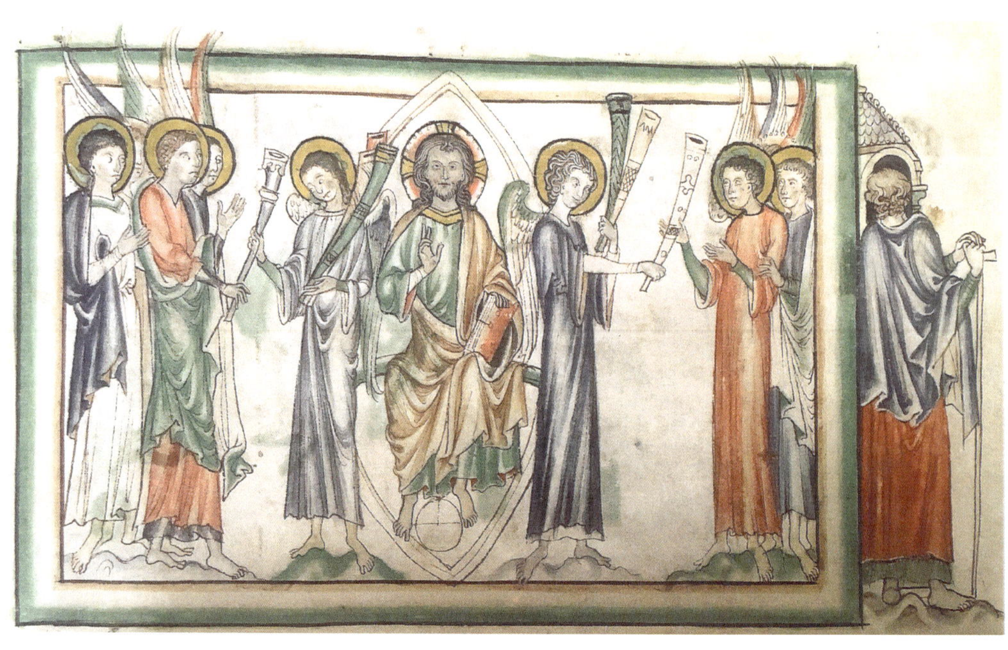

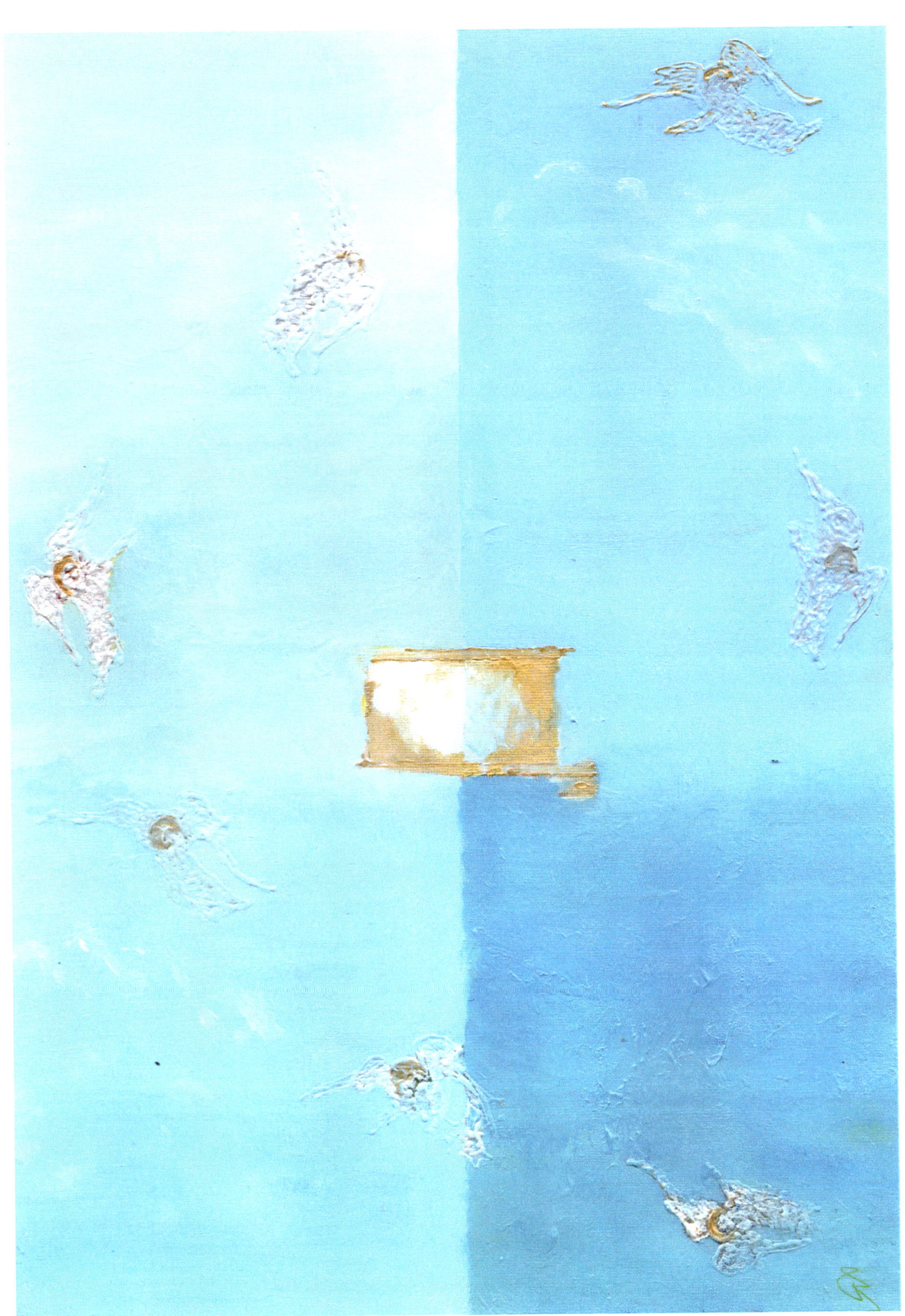

The Scroll is Open at Last

Reading the narrative from beginning to end, the fact that the scroll can now at last be "read" seems significant. Many commentators see the seals, as they are being opened, already revealing what is in the scroll. And a good case is made for that, for example by Caird and others.

I do not get that sense when I read about the opening of the seals. Only when you read the trumpets and bowls backwards into the seals, as many scholars (for example, Tom Wright) do, telling us that the three sevens are merely different versions of the same event, does that make sense. But it is my understanding that you can only say so by reading backwards. In that context it bothers me that the opening of the seventh seal sort of merges with the seven trumpets, and that the trumpets go on to introduce the real action. As Lenski notes, "Seals hide and must be opened in order to reveal; *trumpets* signal, announce, but not until they are blown. *Bowls* contain in order to empty their contents. The order of these could not be changed." Apart from the entrance of the white horse, the opening of the seals did not show much action. [The activity of the horsemen, released as the seals were opened, will become clearer as we read on, culminating in Rev 19 with the white Rider!]

Instead, I have set out to tell the story of Revelation from beginning to end, and the narrative reads perfectly well sequentially, though that does not mean it is also chronological. Time, and particularly exactly when what happens, seems pretty much hidden from our understanding, as Jesus indicated it would be. In any case, heaven and earth work according to different time scales, or so it seems. Some suggest there is no time in heaven.

But now the scroll is open, and it is ready to be read ... so the scroll's contents can become the reality of the early church, and through their testimony would be passed on, till today, even to us. I have certainly seen the four "horses", released with the opening of the first four seals, at work in our twenty-first century! We hear cries of martyrs, every day, and read about the "fulfilled" lives of brothers and sisters in many parts of the world. While Christ is indeed shaking our world, He is also growing His church in previously unimaginable places.

In my painting I show all the opened seals on the edges. I show the four horses, the Lamb who opened the scroll, and the altar. The seal that marked the 144,000 is left intact as the stars fall on the inhabitants of the earth. And behind the "bow" of the rainbow, there is a glimmer of hope, the new Jerusalem in answer to the martyrs' cry.

And I show the open scroll!

What is in the scroll? We are still not told. And we need to patiently read on to find out. The text does give us an indication, with the silence creating a moment of dramatic anticipation. What will be disclosed next? It makes us eager to hurry up and read on!

Is it important? Yes, it is. The prospect of not reading it made John cry! One man received it from the hand of God, and only one was found worthy to open it. So yes, it is very important. And we now expect this scroll to be read, the scroll of the King.

What does the open scroll mean? That Christ and His work will be shown and known in all its fullness, with no secrets, no shadows. Christ is revealed, unveiled, as He has promised in 1:1.

Next, the visions unleashed by the opening of the seals have shown that the revelation of Jesus seriously concerns both heaven and earth. Something happens first in heaven and then on earth (Leithart). But remember, as Ellul reminds us, that the work of Christ – his incarnation, his life, his crucifixion and resurrection – only ever happened on earth. And in that way, what happens on earth also affects heaven and the powers in heaven, as we read in Colossians 2:15: "He disarmed the rulers and authorities and made a public example of them, triumphing over them in it."

At this point heaven is waiting with bated breath. The church is sealed. This apparently was a pre-condition for the scroll to be fully unsealed. And the process of unsealing released powerful visions in which the inhabitants of the earth are urged (shaken) to repent, before the "scroll" of the sky is rolled up!

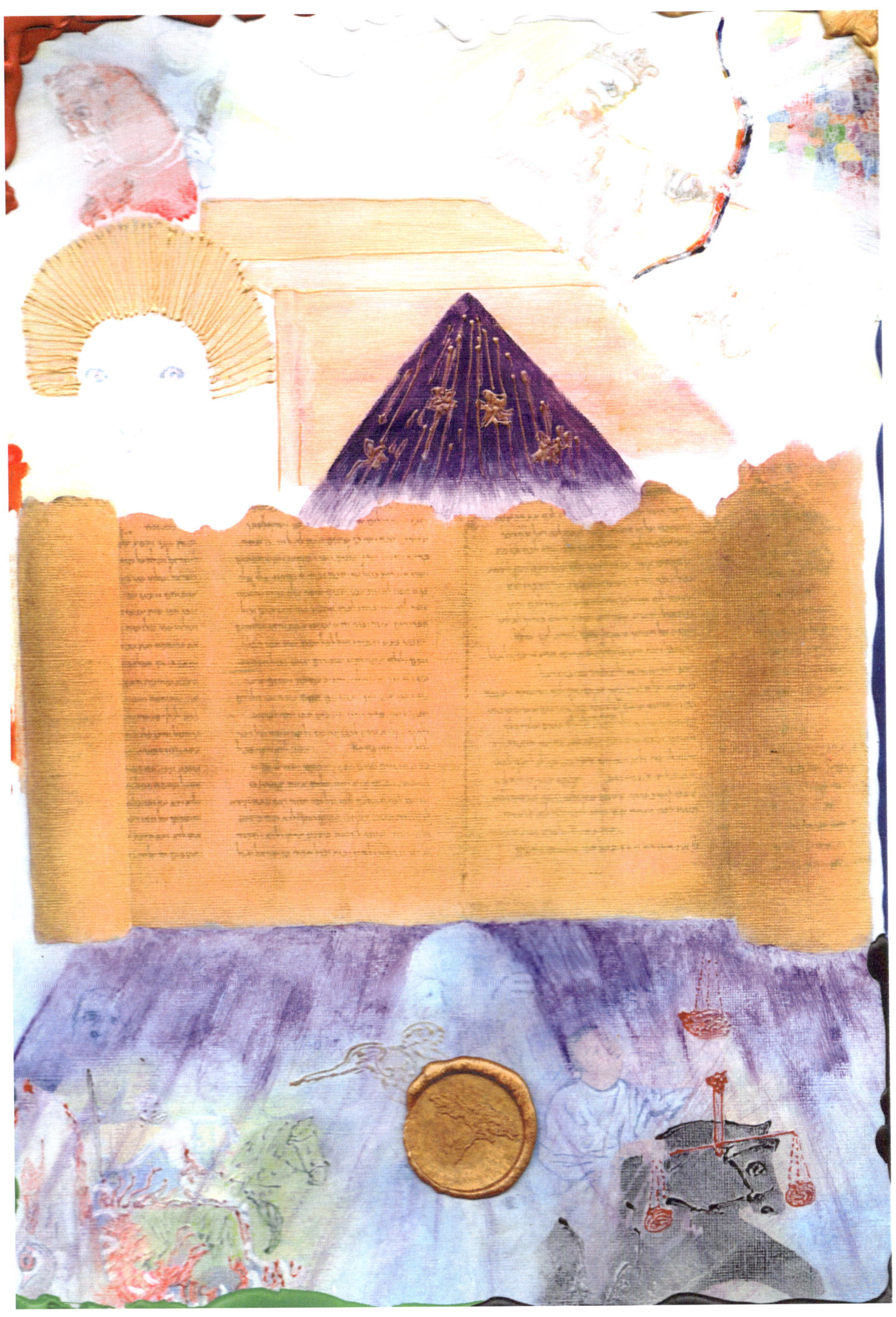

My Understanding of the Seven Seals

As a publisher my first question of any manuscript is: who is this for? Who are the intended readers? Revelation 4–8:1 is a prophecy clearly directed to the seven churches: they are its first hearers. With this in mind we should expect these chapters to be related to them, and this is what we find.

John is in heaven and sees God on His throne in majestic control of His realm, with His council of power around Him worshipping Him. John sees Jesus, the Worthy one, revealed as the Lion of Judah, the Root of David and the Lamb-as-if-it-had-been-slaughtered. Jesus has the same names as God and to Him belongs the seven-fold "blessing and glory and wisdom and thanksgiving and honor and power and might!" He has seven horns and seven eyes, the seven spirits that are sent out into all the world.

The opening of the seals is a prophetic word to the churches to help them understand what was happening at that time and what would happen soon, in their relationships to one another, the Jews/synagogue and the Roman empire. They had already been instructed that their struggle is not against enemies of flesh and blood, but against rulers, authorities, cosmic powers of darkness and spiritual forces of evil in the heavenly places (Eph 6:12). But they had also been reminded that they are blessed by the God and Father of our Lord Jesus Christ, who has blessed His people in Christ with every spiritual blessing in the heavenly places (Eph 1:3) and raised them with Him, seating them in the heavenly places with Him so that in the ages to come He might show the immeasurable riches of His grace in kindness toward those in Christ Jesus (Eph 2:6–7).

The churches have been told to conquer in the way Christ conquered in a spiritual battle that would often be fought in daily life, in the church and in the state. They had to fight not as lions, but as lambs!

Seal 1: The conquering white horse is revealed as the representative of the gospel. It goes into the world when the first seal is opened, and the churches themselves are the result of its ongoing action. When they make their stand, they are part of its mission. This continues today, whenever the gospel goes out, and will continue until the Parousia. The white horse is visually singled out and "special", for already as it sets out on its energetic conquest the rider is wearing a victor's crown!

The white horse is different from the others in that it conquers without any limits, followed by a trio of horses which can be described as the consequences of the gospel message and with limits set as to what they can achieve.

Seal 2: The opening of the second seal releases the red horse of war and persecution: peace is taken from the earth. Jesus clearly spoke about this: "Do not think that I have come to bring peace to the earth; I have not come to bring peace, but a sword" (Matt 10:34), the very sword that is given to the one seated on the red horse. It happened to the church in Smyrna, through the aggression of those who claimed to be Jews but were not, and to the church in Ephesus by the false teaching of the Nicolaitans. And it continues to happen today, for example when family members break with the religion of their birth or culture to become followers of Christ.

Seal 3: The opening of the third seal reveals a black horse, whose seated one has the scales of justice in his hands to testify against injustice. Wheat and barley are almost out of reach for the poor, but oil and wine are still available. Christians were economically disadvantaged at that time because of their exclusion from the Roman guilds. It put pressure on them to submit to emperor worship or the worship of false gods. This trend has continued throughout history, and it is continuing today with Christians facing institutional persecution in many countries, forced to live "underground" with all the deprivation that brings.

Seal 4: The opening of this seal summons the pale-green horse of death and its realm of Hades. Killings by sword, famine, pestilence and wild animals were used by Ezekiel to warn the people of God what would happen if they continued in disobedience. The churches of Ephesus, Pergamum, Thyatira and Laodicea were all challenged to repent and obey. Today many churches are not aware of or hardened to the ways in which they disobey the gospel. This is a searching message but not one that should frighten us into passivity! Remember how Revelation opened: "I am the living one. I was dead, and see, I am alive forever and ever; and I have the keys of death and of Hades" (1:18). Death and Hades are firmly under the control of Christ. They are powerful, but their power is temporary and limited!

Seal 5: The opening of this seal reveals the intense heart cry (*cri de coeur*) of the martyrs. The churches apparently knew Antipas, martyred in Pergamon. The word "slaughter" closely connects these believers to the Lamb. Ever since then, martyrs have been crying out "How long? When will justice be done and our blood avenged on the inhabitants of the earth/land?" We do not often think about this when we live in relative safety from dire persecution. But the pale-green horse is active in our world, today. And while God's reply to the martyrs' question at that time was to wait a bit longer, he also encouraged them by covering their bloody wounds with robes of pure white ...

Seal 6: The opening of this seal seems to initiate frightening action in answer to the martyrs' prayer. Reminiscent of the OT (Sinai) the earth is "shaken" to such an extent that the inhabitants of earth are faced with the reality of God and His Christ. They are terrified, but are they hiding from Him, still trying to ignore His presence, or will they submit to Him? Therefore, this is not about the final, final day. In Acts we read amazing stories of conversion when people are faced with a traumatic "shaking" and hear about Jesus. The churches were full of people who had come there through this kind of experience. And it continued, and continues, with testimonies of great growth in churches as a result of the often tragic "shakings" in our own time. Lord, make me open to see this as the purpose of your "shakings" in my time!

The opening of the sixth seal continues into a second vision to answer the question Who will be able to stand? God provides safety for His people, symbolized by the four winds being held back. The "already" of our salvation does not preclude martyrdom, but a seal ensures safe passage through the ordeal. A perfect 144,000 divided into twelve "tribes" have been sealed. This includes all who have been grafted in.

The second vision continues into a third one, revealing the church as including both believing Jews and gentiles, a great multitude that no one can count: from every nation, tribe, people and language ... It reminds us of the mystery that was revealed to Peter and Paul (for example, Rom 16:25–26) and directly led to the missionary journeys that gave birth to these churches. This mysterious nature of the church, and its phenomenal growth as a result, continues to defy the world. It has continued and continues today in the most unexpected places.

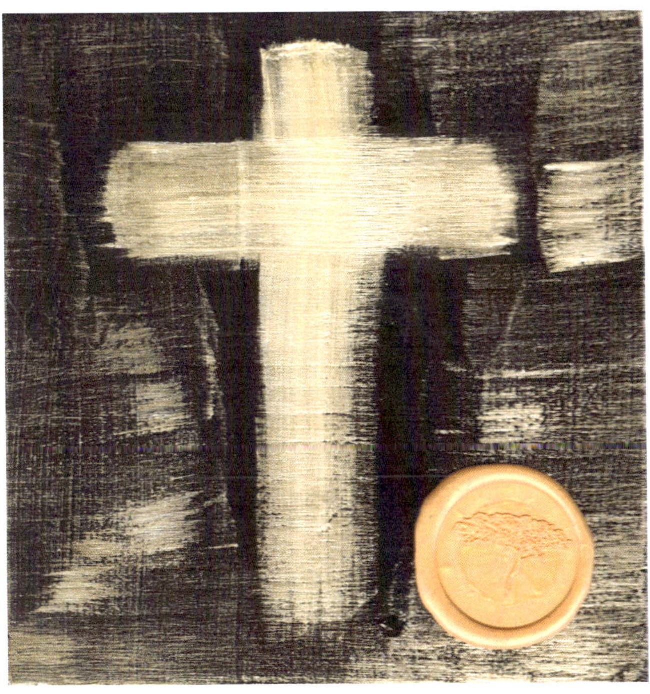

Who are these people? They are those who have come through the great ordeal. Here is a present heavenly reality already enjoyed by those who passed into glory. This is the church in glory, waiting for the final day to unfold.

Seal 7: The opening of the seventh seal is most extraordinary, for it releases silence in heaven! We are entering a new liturgy. To me this proves beyond any doubt that the Parousia has not yet taken place. The story moves on sequentially with a silence (in heaven), worship that includes the incense of the prayers of all the saints (on earth), and the gift of seven trumpets to seven angels that will reveal another "deeper" level of reality. For the churches then it meant that as God tells them to be patient just a bit longer in their suffering, while their prayers continue to be active even when all else is silent in heaven, He gives them a glimpse into the dramatic action happening all the time "behind the scenes". This revelation of a deeper level of meaning attached to the suffering of the church was a reality then (for example Rom 5:3; 1 Pet 4:13), since, and it continues to be the testimony of many believers under extreme pressure today.

Finally, all the seals are open. And then we realize that the activity of opening the seals has not (yet) revealed the content of the scroll! All the focus was on the effort to open it.

We have an open heaven and an open scroll: we have to read on ...

Visual Meditation 2

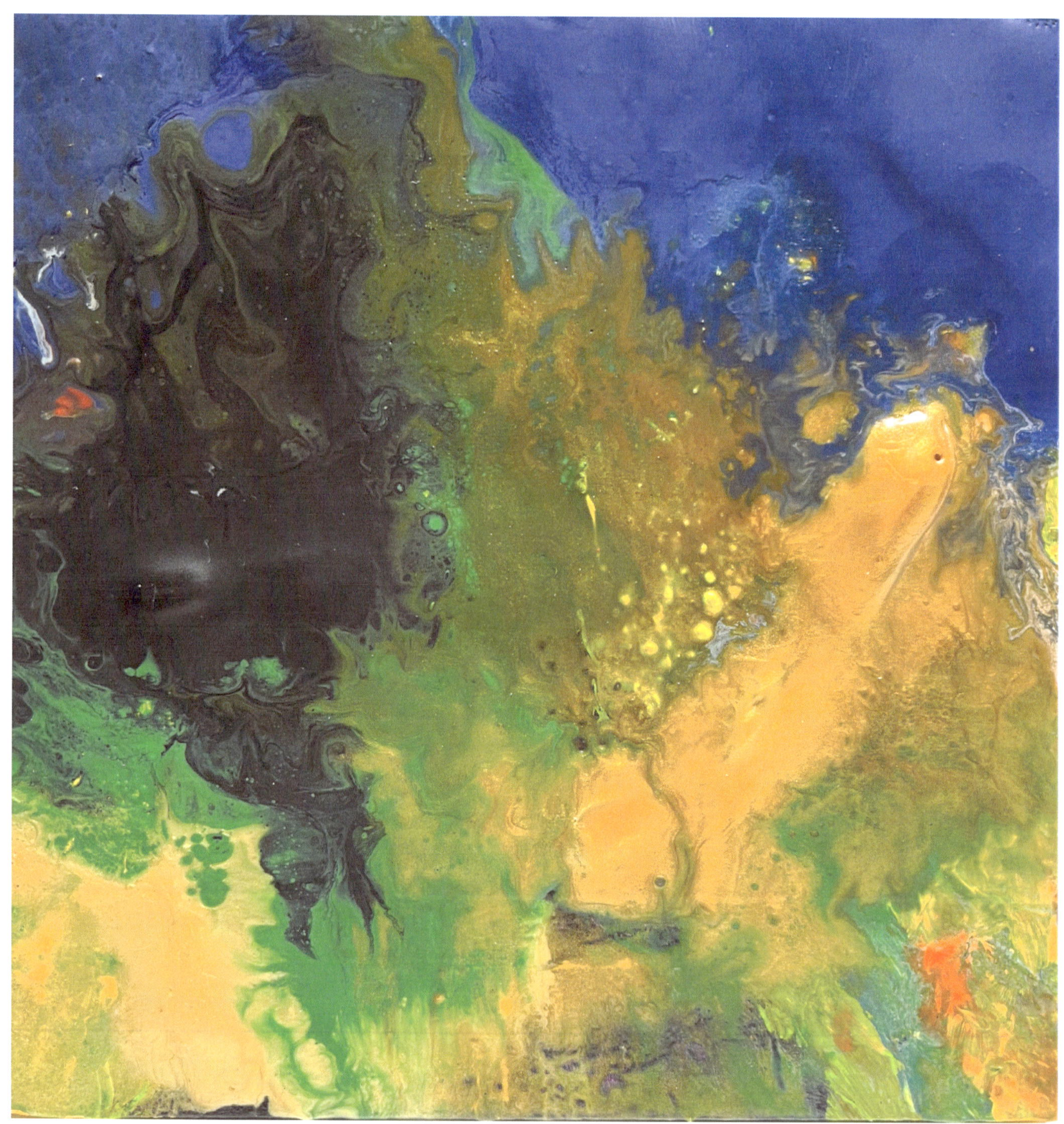

Seal meditation in wax

Additional Select Further Reading

For preachers and church leaders

Hendriksen, William. *More Than Conquerors: An interpretation of the book of Revelation*. Grand Rapids: Baker Pub. Group, 1998.

For serious students and theologians

Beckwith, Isbon Thaddeus. *The Apocalypse of John: studies in introduction, with a critical and exegetical commentary*. Eugene, OR: Wipf & Stock, 2001.

Darko, Daniel K. *Against Principalities and Powers: spiritual beings in relation to communal identity and the moral discourse of Ephesians*. Carlisle UK: Langham Publishing, 2020.

Eaton, Michael A. "Ezekiel" in *The Branch Exposition of the Bible: a preacher's commentary of the Old Testament*. Carlisle UK: Langham Publishing, forthcoming.

Leithart, Peter J. *Deep Exegesis: the mystery of reading scripture*. Baylor University Press, 2020.

Lenski, R. C. H. *The Interpretation of Saint John's Revelation*. Columbus, OH: Lutheran Book Concern, 1935.

Robinson, David Charles. *The Mystic Rules of Scripture: Tyconius of Carthage's keys and windows to the Apocalypse*. Ottawa: Library and Archives Canada = Bibliothèque et Archives Canada, 2011.

Smalley, Stephen S. *Thunder and Love: John's revelation & John's community*. Milton Keynes: Word Pub, 1994.

Smalley, Stephen S. *The Revelation to John: a commentary on the Greek text of the apocalypse*. London: SPCK, 2005.

Stefanovic, Ranko. *Revelation of Jesus Christ: Commentary on the Book of Revelation*, Second Edition. Berrien Springs, MI: Andrews University Press, 2009.

Victorinus of Pettau et al., *Latin Commentaries on Revelation*, ed. William C. Weinrich, Thomas C. Oden, and Gerald L. Bray, trans. William C. Weinrich, Ancient Christian Texts. Downers Grove, IL: IVP Academic: An Imprint of InterVarsity Press, 2011.

For art lovers: books and articles on the precious stones

Bolman, J. *De edel- en siersteenen: indeeling – benamingen – kenmerken – vindplaatsen – herkenning*. Amsterdam, Paris, 1938.

Bolman, J. *De Edelsteenen uit den Bijbel gezien in het licht der hedendaagsche Edelsteenkunde*. Amsterdam, Paris, 1938.

Clapton, E. *The Precious Stones of the Bible: descriptive and symbolical, being a treatise on the breast plate of the high priest, and the foundation of the new Jerusalem with a brief history of each tribe and each apostle*, 2nd Edition. London: Simpkin, 1899.

Cooper, Charles W. "Some of the Precious Stones of the Bible with Special Reference to the High Priest's Breastplate and the Jasper of Revelation." *Journal of the Transactions of The Victoria Institute*, Vol LXI (1929) pp. 4:3, London.

Crowe, Judith. *The Jeweller's Directory of Gemstones: a complete guide to appraising and using precious stones, from cut and colour to shape and setting*. London: Herbert Press, 2006.

Flinders Petrie, W. M. "Stones, Precious." In ed. James Hastings. *A Dictionary of the Bible*, Vol 4. (1899-1904) pp. 619–21. Edinburgh: T&T Clark.

Garber and Funk. "Jewels and Precious Stones." In ed. G. A. Buttrick. *The Interpreter's Dictionary of the Bible: an illustrated encyclopedia* (Nashville: Abingdon, 1962) pp. 898–905.

Gilmore, E. L. "Which Were the Original Twelve Gemstones of the First Biblical Breastplate?" *The Lapidary Journal* 22 (1968) pp. 1130–34.

Harrell, James K. *Bulletin for Biblical Research*, Vol 27.1 (2017) pp. 1–52.

Harrell, James K. *Bulletin for Biblical Research*, Vol 21.2 (2011) pp. 141–71.

Harris, J. S. "The Stones of the High Priest's Breastplate." *The Annual of Leeds University Oriental Society* 5 (1963–65) pp. 40–62.

Harris, J. S. "An Introduction to the Study of Personal Ornaments of Precious, Semi-Precious and Imitation Stones Used throughout Biblical History." *The Annual of Leeds University Oriental Society* 4 (1962–1963) pp. 49–83.

King, C. W. *Antique Gems: their origin, uses, and value as interpreters of ancient history; and as illustrative of ancient art: with hints to gem collectors*. London: J. Murray, 1866.

Patrick, James. "Jewels and Precious Stones." In ed. James Hastings, *A Dictionary of the Bible* (1899–1909).

Patrick, J., and G. R. Driver. "Jewels and Precious Stones." In eds. J. Hastings, F. C. Grant and H. H. Rowley, *Dictionary of the Bible* (New York: Scribner's, 1963) pp. 496–500.

Schumann, Walter. *Gemstones of the World*. New York: Sterling, 2013.

List of Illustrations and References

Paintings by Pieter Kwant

Paintings by other artists

Table of Contents

www.ingramcontent.com/pod-product-compliance
Lightning Source LLC
LaVergne TN
LVRC090924100826
845154LV00013B/160

* 9 7 8 1 8 0 3 2 9 0 0 3 4 *